1

BANGKOK
TRAVEL GUIDE 2023

**The Most Up-to-date Guide For
First Timers Planning a Trip to
Bangkok. Uncover the Rich Culture,
Top attractions, and Hidden Gems —
With Insider Tips and Itineraries.**

By

Harry Gilmore

Table of Contents

My Most Recent Trip to Bangkok

Bangkok has always held a special allure for me, with its rich heritage, breathtaking temples, and tantalizing cuisine. I recently embarked on a whirlwind journey to experience the very best of Bangkok's top attractions, immerse myself in its vibrant culture, and indulge in its delectable culinary delights. Allow me to share the highlights of my enchanting trip to this beautiful city.

As I stepped onto the bustling streets of Bangkok, a familiar sense of excitement washed over me. Having visited this enchanting city before, I knew that another incredible adventure awaited.

This time, I chose to stay in the vibrant neighborhood of Thong Lo, drawn to its modernity and lively ambiance. As I roamed through the stylish cafes and boutique shops, I felt a connection with the city's unique blend of tradition and contemporary flair.

My first stop was the iconic Grand Palace, a place that always left me in awe of its architectural splendor and rich history. Capturing every intricate detail on my camera, I was determined to preserve these cherished memories forever.

Exploring the picturesque canals of Thonburi was an absolute delight. The long-tail boat glided gracefully through the waterways, revealing traditional stilt houses and a serene side of Bangkok that captivated my heart.

Of course, no visit to Bangkok is complete without indulging in its delectable cuisine. I savored the flavors of Pad Thai, Tom Yum Goong, and other mouthwatering dishes, finding pure joy in the diverse and aromatic Thai food.

One evening, I embraced the city's modernity by venturing to Asiatique Riverfront. The lively night market, adorned with colorful lights, offered a vibrant atmosphere and a variety of entertainment options. The lively Muay Thai performance left me in awe, and I couldn't resist exploring the unique handicrafts at the stalls.

As my time in Bangkok drew to a close, I realized that each visit only fueled my passion for this incredible city. Its warm hospitality, rich culture, and vibrant energy made it a place I would always return to with open arms.

With a heavy heart, I bid farewell to Bangkok, knowing that this wouldn't be my last encounter with its allure. As I boarded the plane, I felt grateful for the memories I had created and excited for the future adventures that awaited in this captivating city I held dear to my heart.

Introduction to Bangkok

Bangkok, the captivating capital of Thailand, is a city that exudes an aura of exoticism. Not only is it a bustling hub for Southeast Asia, but it also stands as an alluring destination in its own right. With its vibrant nightlife, delectable cuisine, historical temples, and bustling markets, Bangkok offers a diverse array of experiences that can captivate even the most seasoned travelers.

While many visitors only spend a night or two in the city before venturing to other regions of Thailand, those who choose to linger in Bangkok are in for a treat. The city provides authentic glimpses into Thai life, with neighborhoods and markets designed for locals rather than tourists. Exploring these areas grants you a genuine understanding of everyday life in this dynamic country.

For those who scratch beneath the surface, Bangkok unveils a different side beyond its bustling exterior. The city boasts charming canals adorned with homes and temples, presenting a picturesque sight around every corner. In addition to the well-known tourist temples, Bangkok's residential neighborhoods harbor more intimate and captivating places of worship that are integral to the local way of life.

Furthermore, Bangkok's markets are a treasure trove of unique culinary delights, beautiful fabrics, and reasonably priced souvenirs, untainted by excessive markups. Embracing the art of bargaining is essential in this vibrant city, where you can find great bargains while engaging in the age-old tradition of haggling.

In essence, Bangkok holds more than meets the eye. Beyond the perceived chaotic capital lies a city that thrives with authentic experiences and cultural richness. Whether you indulge in the electrifying nightlife or explore the lesser-known nooks, Bangkok is sure to leave an indelible mark on every traveler who takes the time to discover its true essence.

Having traveled to Bangkok countless times, it feels like a second home to me, and its charm has made it the most visited city in the world for the past four years. Regardless of your background or interests, Bangkok is sure to captivate you with its diverse offerings.

For those embarking on their first journey to Thailand, this comprehensive and Up-to-date Bangkok travel guide aims to assist you in planning an unforgettable trip.

Brief History of Bangkok

Bangkok, the vibrant and bustling capital of Thailand, has a rich and fascinating history that dates back centuries. Its story involves the rise and fall of ancient kingdoms, colonial influences, and a journey towards becoming the modern metropolis it is today.

The area where Bangkok is located has been inhabited since the prehistoric times, with evidence of settlements dating back to the Bronze Age. However, the city as we know it today began to take shape during the 15th century when it was established as a small trading post during the Ayutthaya Kingdom.

In 1767, the Ayutthaya Kingdom fell to the Burmese invaders, leading to the destruction of the city. A new era began when General Taksin, a military leader, successfully drove out the Burmese and established Thonburi as the new capital in 1769. However, his reign was short-lived, and in 1782, General Chao Phraya Chakri (later known as King Rama I) moved the capital across the river to the eastern bank, marking the foundation of present-day Bangkok.

Under the Chakri Dynasty, Bangkok flourished and developed into a major center of culture, trade, and politics. The kings of the Chakri Dynasty were instrumental in modernizing the city and introducing various reforms. During the 19th century, King Rama IV and King Rama V furthered these efforts by embracing Western ideas and technology, helping Thailand maintain its independence amidst European colonial expansion.

Despite this, Thailand was not entirely unaffected by colonialism. The country faced territorial pressure from European powers and had to make certain concessions. However, it managed to remain the only Southeast Asian country never to be fully colonized.

In the 20th century, Bangkok continued to evolve rapidly. The city's infrastructure developed, modern buildings were constructed, and transportation networks expanded. It became a major hub for commerce, attracting both local and international businesses.

In recent decades, Bangkok has faced challenges related to urbanization, population growth, and traffic congestion. Nonetheless, it remains a dynamic and cosmopolitan city, drawing millions of tourists each year with its diverse offerings of cultural landmarks, vibrant street life, delectable cuisine, and lively nightlife.

The history of Bangkok is a captivating tale of resilience, adaptability, and transformation, and its journey from a trading post to a global metropolis showcases the enduring spirit of Thailand's capital city.

Religion Practiced in Bangkok

The most popular religion in Bangkok is Buddhism, which is followed by about 95% of the city's population. There are also significant Christian, Muslim, and Hindu minorities in Bangkok.

Buddhism is the official religion of Thailand, and it has a profound influence on the city's culture and way of life. Buddhist temples are found all over Bangkok, and they are important centers of religious and cultural activity. The most famous Buddhist temple in Bangkok is Wat Pho, which is home to the reclining Buddha, one of the largest Buddha images in the world.

Christianity is the second most popular religion in Bangkok, and it is followed by about 5% of the city's population. The majority of Christians in Bangkok are Catholic, but there are also significant Protestant and Evangelical minorities. There are many Christian churches in Bangkok, and they offer a variety of religious services and programs.

Islam is the third most popular religion in Bangkok, and it is followed by about 4% of the city's population. The majority of Muslims in Bangkok are Sunni, but there is also a small Shia minority. There are many mosques in Bangkok, and they offer a variety of religious services and programs.

Hinduism is the fourth most popular religion in Bangkok, and it is followed by about 1% of the city's population. The majority of Hindus in Bangkok are from India, but there are also significant Thai and Burmese Hindu minorities. There are many Hindu temples in Bangkok, and they offer a variety of religious services and programs.

In addition to these four major religions, there are also a number of smaller religious groups in Bangkok, including Sikhs, Jains, and Baha'is. Bangkok is a tolerant and welcoming city, and people of all faiths are free to practice their religion without fear of discrimination.

Cultural Background

Bangkok's cultural background is deeply rooted in the history and traditions of Thailand. The city serves as the country's cultural, political, and economic center, showcasing a blend of ancient heritage and modern influences.

Monarchy

The Thai monarchy has played a vital role in shaping the country's culture and identity. The Chakri Dynasty, which originated in Bangkok in the late 18th century, continues to reign, and the Thai people hold deep respect and reverence for their kings and the royal family.

Traditional Arts
Bangkok celebrates a wide range of traditional arts, including dance, music, and crafts. Classical Thai dance forms, such as Khon and Ram Thai, are performed on various occasions, showcasing the elegance and grace of Thai culture.

Festivals
Festivals are an essential part of Bangkok's cultural fabric. The most prominent among them is Songkran, the Thai New Year celebration in April, marked by water splashing and various cultural events. Loy Krathong, the Festival of Lights, is another significant event where people release small floats adorned with candles and flowers into rivers and waterways.

Culinary Heritage
Thai cuisine is renowned worldwide for its bold flavors and aromatic spices. Bangkok's street food scene is particularly famous, offering a diverse array of dishes that tantalize the taste buds and reflect the country's regional culinary traditions.

Floating Markets

Bangkok's proximity to waterways has given rise to floating markets, such as Damnoen Saduak and Amphawa, which provide a glimpse into traditional Thai commerce and lifestyle.

Traditional Clothing

The traditional Thai clothing for women, the "chut thai," and for men, the "chong kraben," are still worn on special occasions and cultural events, showcasing the country's sartorial heritage.

Modern Culture

Bangkok's cultural scene is not just limited to its ancient roots. The city has embraced modern influences from around the world, making it a hub for contemporary arts, music, fashion, and entertainment.

Chapter 1

Planning Your Trip to Bangkok

Best Times to Visit Bangkok

Bangkok is a year round destination, offering different experiences depending on the time of year. For those seeking pleasant weather, the period from November to February is considered the best time to visit. During these months, the weather is relatively cooler and mostly sunny, making it ideal for sightseeing and exploring the city's attractions.

On the other hand, if you are budget-conscious and don't mind occasional showers, the rainy season from June to October offers significant discounts on accommodations and activities. It's the most affordable time to plan a trip to Bangkok.

To immerse yourself in the vibrant Thai culture and partake in top festivals, consider visiting in April or November. April hosts the renowned Thai New Year, also known as Songkran Festival, where the city transforms into a massive water fight, offering a fun and joyous experience. November is dedicated to Loy Krathong, another captivating festival celebrated with floating lanterns and boat processions.

The Worst Times to Visit Bangkok

Keep in mind that Bangkok's tropical climate can be unforgiving on certain days. If you are not comfortable with scorching heat and humidity, it's best to avoid visiting in April and May, when temperatures soar.

Similarly, if you dislike rainy weather, plan your trip to Bangkok away from September to early October, as it marks the rainiest period. However, during these less favorable times, you'll find attractive prices and fewer crowds at various attractions.

To make the most of your visit and minimize the impact of heat, it's advisable to organize your schedule wisely. The late afternoon and early evening are when rain typically occurs, so planning indoor activities or taking a break during these times can be a smart choice.

Month by Month Weather in Bangkok

May to October, specifically March to May, represents the hottest months in Bangkok, with temperatures often exceeding 40°C (104°F). While the weather might not be the most comfortable,

April offers the lively Songkran Festival, making it an exciting time to be in the city.

November to February brings the dry and cooler climate, making it the ideal time to explore Bangkok. However, this peak tourist season might result in slightly higher prices and larger crowds.

From June to October, the rainy season sets in, lasting until the beginning of November. During this time, Bangkok experiences fewer visitors, creating a more tranquil atmosphere.

Entry Requirements and Visa Information

Before traveling to Thailand, it is essential to check your eligibility and visa requirements. General travelers have the option of entering Thailand without a visa under the Visa Exemption program. For those visiting Thailand for a holiday, a "Visa on arrival" is available. However, individuals with different purposes of stay must obtain a Thai visa from their local Thai Embassy or Consulate before arrival.

To obtain a visa on arrival in Bangkok, you must meet specific criteria:

1. Be a citizen of a country eligible for a visa on arrival.
2. Possess a valid passport with at least 6 months of validity from the arrival date.
3. Show a confirmed hotel reservation in Thailand.
4. Hold a return or onward ticket from Thailand.
5. Pay a visa on arrival fee of 2,000 baht (approximately $60).

If you are ineligible for a visa on arrival, you should apply for a visa at a Thai embassy or consulate in your home country. Requirements for visas vary depending on nationality, so it's advisable to check with the Thai embassy or consulate for relevant information.

Visa Exemption

Visa Exemption allows citizens of certain countries to enter Thailand for tourism purposes for up to 30 days. These countries include various ASEAN nations and others such as Australia, Canada, Japan, the United States, and many European countries.

Covid-19 requirements:

As of March 8, 2023, all travelers entering Thailand must be fully vaccinated against COVID-19 and provide a negative COVID-19 test result taken within 72 hours of their flight.

Essential Packing List for Bangkok: 9 Must-Have Items

In addition to the essential travel items like weather-appropriate clothing, medicine, toiletries, phone, and camera, here's a comprehensive guide on what to pack for your trip to Bangkok.

1. Tissue and Wet Wipes
Thai toilets often lack toilet paper and soap, and toilet seat cleaners are rare. To maintain good hygiene, pack both tissue and wet wipes. They'll prove to be invaluable, especially when trying out delicious Thai street food during your adventures.

2. Appropriate Clothing for Temples and Palaces
As you likely have at least one temple visit on your Thailand itinerary, dressing appropriately is crucial. For places like the Grand Palace and Wat Phra Kaew (Temple of the Emerald Buddha), both men and women must wear sleeved clothes, covering their shoulders, ankles, and midriff. Men are required to wear long trousers, while women should opt for long trousers or skirts. Avoid tight pants and flip-flops.

While other temples may have slightly relaxed rules, avoid revealing clothing as a sign of respect.

3. Slip-On Shoes

Many places, including temples, require visitors to remove their shoes. Opt for slip-on shoes to make this process more convenient. Sandals are a great option too, but in the rainy season, avoid those with plastic soles to prevent slipping.

4. Sun Protection

Bangkok's sunlight can be intense, so be sure to pack a hat, sunglasses, and sunscreen to protect yourself from the strong rays.

5. Rain Gear

Even during the colder months (November to February), there's a chance of rain in Bangkok. Bring an umbrella or raincoat to stay dry and prepared.

6. Insect Repellent

Bangkok's tropical and rainy nature makes it important to pack insect repellent, especially if you plan to camp or trek.

7. Water Bottle

Staying hydrated is essential in Bangkok's hot climate. Although tap water isn't drinkable, many accommodations provide free drinking water. Avoid overpriced bottled water at tourist attractions by carrying your own reusable water bottle.

8. Power Adapter for Bangkok

For your electronic devices, ensure you have a 220v power adapter suitable for Bangkok's power outlets.

9. Tourist SIM Card

Embrace the convenience of mobile apps like Grab and Uber to avoid taxi scams and explore the city on foot using Google Maps. Access useful information on the go, keep in touch with your loved ones, and enjoy a seamless experience by booking a tourist SIM card in advance, as Wi-Fi may only be available at accommodations and select restaurants and cafés.

Getting to Bangkok

Getting to Bangkok provides two international airport options - Suvarnabhumi Airport (BKK) and Don Mueang Airport (DMK).

Suvarnabhumi Airport (BKK) serves as the primary airport with a greater number of international flights, making it the primary entry point for most tourists visiting Bangkok.

To reach downtown Bangkok from Suvarnabhumi International Airport, you have two convenient options:

By Train
The most recommended way is to take the Airport Rail Link from Suvarnabhumi to Phaya Thai Station, which costs THB 45. From there, you can easily transfer to the BTS line and reach the station closest to your hotel. You can buy tickets at the station.

By Bus

Alternatively, you can board the S1 bus departing from Gate 7 on the first floor of the passenger terminal, which will take you directly to Khaosan Road. The fare for this bus ride is THB 60, and it operates every 30 minutes from 6 AM to 8 PM.

From Suvarnabhumi International Airport (BKK), you have various transportation choices to reach downtown Bangkok.

Taxi or Grab

Taking a taxi or Grab to downtown Bangkok typically costs around THB 400, including the airport surcharge and toll. To avoid scams, ensure the driver uses the meter, as taxi scams are unfortunately common in the City.

Private Ride

Although it's the priciest option, a private ride provides convenience and comfort. You can book private transfers from Suvarnabhumi International Airport (BKK) to downtown Bangkok .

Don Mueang International Airport (DMK)

Moving on to Don Mueang International Airport (DMK), there are also several ways to get to downtown Bangkok.

Train

As Don Mueang lacks a BTS or MRT station, you'll have to rely on a bus or taxi to reach the closest train station, Mo Chit. To catch the A1 bus to Mo Chit BTS Station, exit the terminal, and the fare is THB 30, with buses running approximately every 15 minutes between 7:30 AM and 11:30 PM. Once at Mo Chit Station, you can continue your journey via the BTS to the station closest to your hotel.

Bus

Another option is to board the A2, A3, or A4 bus from Don Mueang to various destinations. The A2 bus goes to Victory Monument, A3 to Pratunam and Lumpini Park, and A4 to Khao San Road and Sanam Luang. Bus fares range from THB 30 to THB 50, and the buses operate every 30 minutes from 7:30 AM to 11:30 PM. Note that buses can get crowded, so it might be more convenient to take the bus to Mo Chit and continue the journey by train.

Taxi or Grab

Opting for a taxi or Grab ride from Don Mueang to downtown Bangkok should cost you around THB 350, including the airport surcharge and toll. Remember to insist on the driver using the meter to avoid any issues.

Private Ride

Similar to Suvarnabhumi Airport, a private ride is a comfortable yet expensive choice for transportation from Don Mueang Airport to downtown Bangkok.

Getting Around Bangkok: Efficient Transportation Options

Bangkok, being a vast metropolis, can be time-consuming to get around. Therefore, carefully choosing your base location when visiting is recommended.

Thankfully, the public transportation system has seen significant improvements in recent years.

BTS Skytrain / MRT

I appreciate cities with excellent metro systems like Seoul and Taipei, as they efficiently connect various areas. While Bangkok's BTS and MRT Lines are modern and well-functioning, their coverage is not as extensive. Often, I found myself taking the train to the nearest subway stop and then either walking or using Grab to reach my final destination. You might encounter a similar situation.

Grab

As mentioned, you'll likely need alternative transportation to complement the subway system. Despite appearing slightly more expensive than taxis, I strongly advocate for using Grab.

Taxi and tuk-tuk scams are prevalent in Bangkok, and I've personally fallen victim to such incidents in the past, leaving me disenchanted with these options.

Ferry

Escaping the traffic and exploring Bangkok alongside locals can be a delightful experience by utilizing the river ferries. Many of the city's attractions are located along the Chao Phraya River, and both local and express ferries operate frequently throughout the day. Additionally, smaller canal ferries provide access to other areas.

Taxi

Opting for an air-conditioned taxi may seem appealing, but Bangkok's traffic jams are notorious and frequent. Taxis can often become trapped in gridlock for extended periods. While it may be the only option on certain occasions, my preference is to use the Grab app (similar to Uber) for booking and payment convenience.

Tuk-Tuks

Thailand's iconic three-wheelers are a fun way to travel around the city, but they are best avoided during rush hours. Being stuck behind an exhaust-guzzling bus in traffic is not an enjoyable experience. Before getting in, be sure to agree on a price and be prepared to haggle.

Best Neighborhoods To Stay In Bangkok

Selecting the right neighborhood for your stay in Bangkok can be a daunting task, considering the city's size and the limited coverage of the subway system, despite its convenience.

To ensure easy access to transportation and reduce reliance on taxis or Grab, I recommend staying in a commercial area near a BTS or MRT station. This allows for seamless exploration of the city using public transport.

Downtown Bangkok boasts eight popular tourist lodging areas: **Sukhumvit, Siam, Silom, Pratunam, Riverside, Chinatown, the Old City (Rattanakosin), and Chatuchak.** Additionally, due to the notorious rush hour traffic, some international tourists prefer accommodations near Suvarnabhumi Airport, making it the ninth option.

For first-time visitors, the Siam or Sukhumvit areas are ideal choices, offering a perfect combination of shopping, food, and easy transportation.

SUKHUMVIT

Sukhumvit is renowned for its cosmopolitan vibe, attracting foreigners and expats. It hosts luxury hotels, a plethora of restaurants with diverse cuisines, and a vibrant nightlife centered around Soi 11, one of Bangkok's famous party streets. Both the BTS and MRT lines run through Sukhumvit, ensuring hassle-free commuting.

On the other hand, if shopping is your primary focus, Siam is the perfect neighborhood for you. Filled with shopping centers, department stores, boutiques, restaurants, cafes, and bars, Siam promises a shopper's paradise. Staying here ensures easy access to the BTS Skytrain, facilitating convenient transportation.

PRATUNAM

For those seeking a memorable shopping experience, Pratunam is a fantastic choice. Baiyoke Sky Hotel, Southeast Asia's tallest hotel at 88 storeys, offers spectacular city views. The area is close to air-conditioned shopping malls like MBK, Siam Center, and Siam Paragon in the Siam area. The BTS and MRT lines make exploring Pratunam and its surroundings hassle-free.

Whichever neighborhood you choose, each offers unique experiences and easy access to Bangkok's attractions, ensuring a delightful and convenient stay in this vibrant city.

SILOM

Silom, Bangkok's business district, offers another popular area to stay. While not as bustling as Siam and Sukhumvit, Silom has its charm with attractions like Lumphini Park, the Patpong night market, and the infamous Patpong red light district. Both the BTS and MRT lines serve Silom, making commuting a breeze.

CHINATOWN

For food enthusiasts seeking delectable street eats, Chinatown emerges as a top-notch destination. Yaowarat Road, the vibrant heart of Chinatown, boasts some of the best and most famous street food stalls in Bangkok.

Yet, amidst the culinary delights, Chinatown can be a hectic area and may not be the best fit for those seeking a more tranquil stay in the city. Furthermore, with only two MRT stations serving the neighborhood, transportation options are relatively limited

RIVERSIDE

Nestled along the serene Chao Phraya River, the Riverside area exudes a relaxed and upscale ambiance. I chose an AirBnB at Ideo Mobi Sathorn for my stay. It is a residential condominium conveniently located near Krung Thonburi BTS station.

What made this neighborhood appealing was its distance from the bustling chaos of downtown Bangkok. However, being slightly far from the city's commercial areas meant a daily commute to access them. While it's a wonderful place to stay, it might not be the most suitable choice for first-time visitors to Bangkok.

CHATUCHAK

Located not far from the Chatuchak Weekend Market, the Centara Grand at Central Plaza Ladprao offers luxurious and comfortable 5-star accommodation. The hotel may not be the most modern, but its array of excellent restaurants, including the delightful Suan Bua Thai Restaurant, enhances the overall experience.

Chatuchak is situated a bit farther from the city's major attractions, making it a suitable choice for travelers whose main objective is to indulge in shopping at the Chatuchak Weekend Market or those needing proximity to Don Mueang Airport.

THE OLD CITY

Khaosan Road, described as "the center of the backpacking universe" in the movie "The Beach" starring Leonardo DiCaprio, characterizes the lively atmosphere of the Old City. This was my go-to neighborhood for solo trips to Bangkok two decades ago. The area is renowned for its plethora of bars, budget-friendly guesthouses, and economical dining options, making it a preferred choice for young backpackers.

If you're a youthful traveler who enjoys the party scene and is on a budget, staying near Khaosan Road is a compelling option. Additionally, the Grand Palace and Wat Pho are easily accessible from this vibrant area. While the Old City used to lack metro stations, the opening of the Sanam Chai MRT station in 2019 has significantly improved transportation convenience, with a mere 5-minute walk to Wat Pho.

SUVARNABHUMI AIRPORT

Staying near Suvarnabhumi Airport is primarily advantageous if you arrive late at night or have an early morning flight to catch. As it is approximately an hour away from downtown Bangkok, Suvarnabhumi Airport isn't an ideal base for exploring the city.

On a previous visit to Thailand, I spent one night at The Cottage, a convenient choice for travelers flying in from Chiang Mai and requiring close proximity to the airport for an early international flight. The Cottage offers a quick 5-minute drive to Suvarnabhumi Airport and is within walking distance of the Paseo Community Mall, featuring an array of restaurants and shops. Additionally, they offer free shuttle transfers to the airport, further enhancing convenience for guests.

CHAPTER 2

PRACTICAL TIPS FOR TRAVELING IN BANGKOK

Money and Currency Exchange

Thailand's official currency is the Thai Baht (THB), symbolized as "฿". Baht is available in both coins and banknotes, with coins in denominations of 1, 2, 5, and 10 Baht, and banknotes in denominations of 20, 50, 100, 500, and 1,000 Baht.

To start your trip, it's advisable to exchange a small amount, not exceeding USD 100, at the airport to cover initial expenses. Alternatively, withdrawing THB from ATMs is a viable option with competitive exchange rates. However, do inform your bank beforehand about your travel plans to avoid any complications. Some ATMs may offer the choice of proceeding "with or without conversion"; always opt for "without conversion" to avoid unfavorable rates set by the foreign bank operating the ATM.

Tipping in Bangkok

While tipping is not customary in Thailand, it is appreciated for exceptional service. In upscale restaurants or when utilizing the services of tour guides or drivers, a gratuity of around 10% is a thoughtful gesture to express gratitude.

Important Tips for First Time Visitors

1. Ensure Reliable Connectivity with Pocket Wifi or SIM Card

Staying connected is essential while traveling, and having a reliable wifi connection makes navigating and researching much easier. Renting a pocket wifi device or purchasing a local SIM card is a convenient way to ensure constant connectivity in Thailand. While we prefer pocket wifi with unlimited data for its simplicity, using a SIM card is a cost-effective alternative. Both options are available through Klook.

2. Respectful Dress Code for Temples and Palaces

When visiting iconic landmarks like the Grand Palace and Bangkok's temples, it's crucial to dress appropriately to show respect for Thai customs and traditions. Observe the following dress code:

- Avoid wearing short skirts, shorts, or shortened trousers. Skirts that fall below the knee are acceptable.

- Tight-fitting trousers or leggings should be avoided.

- Refrain from wearing clothing with holes, such as ripped jeans.

- Tops without sleeves are not permitted, even if covered with a scarf. Always ensure sleeves are rolled down.

- Any form of sportswear, including sweatshirts and sweatpants, is not suitable.

- Although sandals or flip-flops may be acceptable, it is advisable to wear closed shoes for a more appropriate appearance.

3. Consider Travel Insurance

While age may influence your decision, travel insurance is vital for certain trips and activities. For shorter visits focused on street food and night markets, travel insurance might not be necessary. However, if you plan on engaging in adventurous activities like hiking or bike riding, securing a travel insurance policy is highly recommended for peace of mind.

4. Savor Affordable Local Food at Suvarnabhumi Airport

If you're a fan of airport dining, head to the 24-hour food court in Suvarnabhumi Airport's basement before departure. Unlike typical airport fare, this food court offers delicious Thai meals at reasonable prices, allowing you to enjoy one last authentic culinary experience before your journey.

Travel Safety Tips

1. Beware of Scams:

Scams can happen anywhere, and Bangkok is no exception. Stay vigilant and be cautious of the following scams:

Airport Taxi Scam: Avoid unscrupulous taxi drivers offering inflated fares. Use the legitimate metered taxis available at designated queues in Suvarnabhumi or Don Mueang Airport.
Scam of "It's Closed": Be wary of drivers who claim that your destination is closed to divert you to

other establishments where they receive commissions.

Scam from Friendly Local: Beware of strangers posing as helpful locals who might try to take you to gem shops or tailors for personal gain.

2. Cautious with Street Food:
While Bangkok is renowned for its street food, exercise caution when selecting vendors. Choose those with good hygiene practices, and ensure that food is thoroughly cooked and served hot to minimize health risks.

3. Stay Hydrated:
Given Bangkok's hot and humid climate, drink plenty of water to stay hydrated. Stick to bottled or filtered water to avoid drinking tap water.

4. Be Vigilant in Crowded Places:
In crowded areas such as tourist attractions, markets, and public transportation, be attentive to your surroundings to prevent pickpocketing and theft.

5. Choose Safe Accommodations:

Prioritize booking accommodations in safe and reputable areas. Read reviews and assess safety ratings to ensure a secure stay.

Cultural Etiquette in Bangkok

1. Respect Local Customs: When entering someone's home, temples, or certain shops, adhere to Thai customs and remove your shoes. Follow the locals' lead or look for a shoe rack as a signal to take off your shoes.

2. Embrace the Thai Greeting "Wai": Engage in the traditional Thai greeting known as a "wai" to show respect. Press your palms together in a prayer-like gesture and slightly bow. The higher you position your hands, the more respect you convey. If someone offers you a wai, particularly elders or those of higher social status, reciprocate the gesture as a sign of politeness and courtesy.

3. Politeness and Respect: Thai culture greatly values courteous conduct and reverence for their customs and traditions. When engaging with locals, it's appreciated to use expressions like "please" and "thank you" while avoiding any public display of irritation or frustration.

4. Feet and Head: Within Thai customs, the head is regarded as the most sacred part of the body, whereas the feet are seen as the lowest. One should refrain from touching someone's head and avoid pointing their feet or displaying the soles towards people or religious symbols.

5. Public Displays of Affection: Thai society tends to be conservative when it comes to exhibiting affection in public. It's advisable to keep intimate gestures, such as kissing and hugging, private and refrain from excessive public displays of affection.

6. Handling Buddha Images: When visiting temples, it is vital to show respect while taking photographs of Buddha images. Sitting or climbing on Buddha statues should never be done, and one should avoid turning their back to the statue while capturing pictures.

7. Monarchy Respect: Being mindful of conversations related to the Thai monarchy is essential. The Thai people deeply respect their royal family, and any negative remarks or actions can be offensive and may result in legal consequences.

8. Language: Learning a few basic Thai phrases or greetings is a meaningful way to connect with locals. Thai people genuinely appreciate visitors who make an effort to speak their language.

Emergency contacts information

In case of emergencies in Bangkok, remember these important contact numbers:

1. Tourist Police: 1155
Trained to assist tourists, the Tourist Police can help in various situations, including theft, scams, accidents, or emergencies.

2. Police (General Emergency): 191
For any general emergency requiring police assistance, dial 191.

3. Ambulance and Medical Emergencies: 1669
Reach emergency medical services in Bangkok to dispatch an ambulance when immediate medical attention is needed.

4. Fire Department: 199

In case of a fire emergency, dial 199 for the fire department.

5. Tourist Helpline: 1672

The 24/7 Tourist Helpline offers support for general inquiries and travel assistance.

Save these numbers in your phone or write them down for quick access during your stay in Bangkok. Additionally, hotels and tourist areas provide information on local emergency contacts, so don't hesitate to seek help when necessary.

Chapter 3

BANGKOK TRAVEL BUDGET AND COST OF LIVING

Cost of Traveling to Bangkok

On an average *day*, plan to spend approximately ฿2,666 ($77) during your vacation in Bangkok.

For meals, the average cost is ฿645 ($19) per day, and for local transportation, it's ฿180 ($5.19).

The average hotel price for a couple in Bangkok is ฿2,899 ($84), resulting in a one-week trip for two people costing around ฿37,328 ($1,078).

A two-week trip for two people amounts to ฿74,655 in Bangkok. If traveling as a family of three or four, costs can be reduced as children's tickets are cheaper, and hotel rooms can be shared. Longer travel periods also lead to lower daily budgets per person.

How Much Money To Budget For Your Trip

Here's a breakdown of the average Bangkok trip cost by category:

Accommodation Budget

The average price for one person's accommodation in Bangkok is ฿1,450. For two people sharing a double-occupancy hotel room, the average price is ฿2,899.

Transportation Budget

Local transportation in Bangkok costs approximately ฿180 per person per day, with taxis being more expensive than public transportation.

Food Budget

The average daily cost of food in Bangkok is ฿645, with an average meal at a sit-down restaurant costing around ฿258 per person. Breakfast is usually cheaper than lunch or dinner, and street food prices are more affordable than sit-down restaurants.

Entertainment Budget

Entertainment and activities in Bangkok average around ฿505 per person per day, including admission tickets to attractions, day tours, and sightseeing expenses.

How To Save Money While Traveling in Bangkok

Save money during your stay in Bangkok with smart budgeting and savvy spending. Use these tips to make the most of your money.:

1. Accommodation: Look for budget-friendly options like hostels, guesthouses, or budget hotels. Booking in advance and during off-peak seasons often leads to better deals.

2. Street Food: Embrace Bangkok's street food culture for delicious and affordable meals. Popular street food spots offer authentic Thai cuisine at lower costs.

3. Public Transportation: Utilize Bangkok's efficient public transportation, such as the BTS Skytrain, MRT subway, and public buses, which are cheaper than taxis or tuk-tuks.

4. Free and Low-Cost Attractions: Take advantage of free or low-cost attractions, including temples, local markets, public parks, and cultural events.

5. Bargaining: Practice your bargaining skills in local markets to negotiate prices and get better deals.

6. Tuk-tuk and Taxi Fares: Negotiate the fare upfront or insist on using the meter when using tuk-tuks or taxis to avoid overcharging.

7. Water and Snacks: Carry a reusable water bottle and refill it at water stations or request free tap water in restaurants. Buy snacks and drinks from local convenience stores for better prices.

8. Avoid Scams: Be vigilant against common scams targeting tourists, such as overcharging or counterfeit products.

9. Prepaid SIM Card: Purchase a prepaid SIM card with data to stay connected without high roaming charges.

10. Use Travel Apps: Make use of travel apps offering discounts, deals, and coupons for activities, dining, and accommodations in Bangkok.

following these money-saving tips, you can enjoy a budget-friendly trip to Bangkok while indulging in all the city's fantastic experiences.

Chapter 4

HOTELS AND ACCOMMODATION IN BANGKOK

Bangkok boasts a diverse array of accommodation options catering to different preferences and budgets. Whether you seek opulent luxury hotels, charming boutique stays, budget-friendly hostels, or convenient serviced apartments, the city has something to suit every traveler's needs.

Luxury Hotels in Bangkok

Hyatt Regency Bangkok Sukhumvit

Address: 1 Sukhumvit Soi 13 Road,, Klongtoey Nua, Wattana, Wattana, Bangkok..

The Hyatt Regency Bangkok Sukhumvit offers a 5-star experience. Guests can enjoy a range of amenities, including a fitness center, garden, terrace, and bar. The hotel provides free WiFi, room service, and a 24-hour front desk for utmost convenience. Dining options are plentiful, with a restaurant serving American, Steakhouse, and Thai cuisine, along with vegetarian, dairy-free, and halal choices.

Notable attractions such as Emporium Shopping Mall, Central Embassy, and Amarin Plaza are within easy reach.

The St Regis Bangkok

Address: 159 Rajadamri Road, Pathumwan, Bangkok..

The St Regis Bangkok epitomizes elegance. The hotel delights guests with its exquisite Clinique La Prairie Aesthetics & Medical Spa and personalized butler services. The spacious rooms exude warmth through stylish rugs, Thai artwork, and polished wooden flooring. Each room comes with modern amenities such as a flat-screen LED TV and minibar. The large private bathroom boasts double sinks, a soaking tub, and a wall-mounted rain shower. The hotel is conveniently located near Gaysorn Plaza for luxury shopping. Siam Paragon, Central World Plaza, and other attractions are just a short distance away.

W Bangkok Hotel

Address: 106 North Sathorn Road, Silom, Bangrak, Bang Rak, Bangkok..

The W Bangkok Hotel offers contemporary luxury and convenience. Within a 3-minute walk from Chong Nonsi BTS Skytrain Station and Mahanakohn, guests can easily explore the city. The hotel features an outdoor pool, fitness center, and an on-site restaurant. The stylish rooms come equipped with cable flat-screen TVs, iPod docking stations, and refrigerators. The en suite bathrooms offer free toiletries, a bathtub, and shower facilities. The property is located near Silom Road and is approximately 40 minutes from Suvarnabhumi International Airport. Shopping destinations like Siam Paragon Shopping Mall are easily accessible. Guests can also enjoy spa treatments and dining experiences at the hotel's various restaurants.

InterContinental Bangkok

Address: 973 Phloen Chit Road, Pathumwan, Bangkok

The contemporary InterContinental Bangkok Pathumwan provides exquisite accommodations within 200 meters from Chitlom BTS Skytrain Station. It offers relaxing spa treatments, an outdoor pool, and five dining choices.

Within a short 5-minute stroll from the InterContinental Bangkok, you'll find Central World Plaza and Gaysorn Plaza. Suvarnabhumi Airport is 23 kilometers away.

The InterContinental's spacious air-conditioned rooms are stylishly designed and boast huge double-glazed windows with views of the city. Every room is equipped with a flat-screen TV that has cable/satellite channels and a DVD player.

The 24-hour Infinity Fitness offers a bird's eye view over Bangkok as well as a well-equipped gym and yoga courses. Following a revitalizing exercise, visitors may unwind with a massage or facial at Spa InterContinental.

The hotel's restaurants provide a delectable array of foreign, Western, Italian, and Chinese cuisine. The hotel's two bars serve champagne and cigars.

Hotel Royal Bangkok

Address: 409-421/4 Yaowarat road, Bangkok

The Hotel Royal Bangkok at Chinatown in Bangkok has an outdoor salt-water pool, a bar, and a restaurant. Guests have complimentary WiFi access throughout the hotel.

Each air-conditioned room has a flat-screen TV, a safety deposit box, and ironing equipment. There is a desk and an electric kettle accessible. Some flats have a lounge space with a couch or a dining area. The private bathroom has shower amenities as well as a hairdryer and bathrobes. Toiletries are given for free. The Superior Room is the only one without windows.

There is also a fitness center, a tour desk, and baggage storage at Hotel Royal. The 24-hour front desk may arrange airport transfer services. There is also the possibility of free parking.

The lodging is 260 meters from Wat Mangkon MRT Subway Station and 500 meters from Hua Lamphong Train Station in terms of public transportation. Suvarnabhumi International Airport is 36 kilometers distant.

Guests can dine at the hotel's on-site restaurant or unwind at the poolside bar.

Mid Range Hotels in Bangkok

Norn Yaowarat Hotel

6,8,10-12 Padung Dao Rd.,. Samphanthawong, Bangkok..

Norn Yaowarat Hotel is a 4-story building in the center of Bangkok's ChinaTown on PadungDao Road, popularly known as Soi Texas. It offers free WiFi throughout the premises. The distance to Sampeng Market is only 300 meters, and you'll find Wat Mangkon MRT Subway Station just 190 meters away.

Certain rooms include a patio or balcony. There is a flat-screen TV available.

On the first level, guests may enjoy the pudding store. The property offers ticketing services.

Norn Yaowarat Hotel is 1.5 kilometers from Temple of the Golden Mount, while Asiatique the Riverfront open-air mall is 7 kilometers away and may be accessed by vehicle or boat.

Don Mueang International Airport is 22 kilometers away from Norn Yaowarat Hotel, while Suvarnabhumi Airport is accessible through Airport Rail Link and MRT stations.

The Quarter Ladprao

Address: 80 Soi Ladprao 4, Ladprao Road;, Chom Phon, Chatuchak, Chatuchak, Bangkok..

In Bangkok, the Quarter Ladprao offers an outdoor swimming pool, a fitness center, a garden, and a restaurant. This 4-star hotel has room service, a 24-hour front desk, and complimentary WiFi. The hotel is non-smoking and located 1.2 kilometers from Central Plaza Ladprao.

Air conditioning, a sitting area, a flat-screen TV with satellite channels, a safety deposit box, and a private bathroom with a shower, complimentary amenities, and a hairdryer are included in all hotel rooms. Quarter Ladprao also serves an American or Asian breakfast.

The hotel has four stars and a hammam as well as a sun patio.

The Quarter Ladprao is 3.3 kilometers from Chatuchak Weekend Market, while Central Festival EastVille is 8.7 km away. Don Mueang International Airport is 16 kilometers from the hotel.

Old Capital Bike Inn - (SHA Certified)

Address: 609 Pra Sumen Road, Pra Nakhon, Bangkok, Bangkok

The historic Old Capital Bike Inn provides rooms that are uniquely outfitted with antique furniture and many are embellished with hand-painted porcelain and offers free bike and night cycle tours.The motel offers free WiFi throughout.

The hotel is conveniently situated within a 15-minute walking distance from Khao San Road. The Golden Mountain and Pann Fah Pier are a 5-minute walk away.

In each room of The inn, you will find amenities such as air conditioning, satellite TV, and multimedia facilities. An en suite bathroom with free amenities.

The hotel has a 24-hour front desk and baggage storage. A library & laundry facilities are also provided.

The coffee shop in the hotel sells freshly prepared coffee. Breakfast is served in the room. The property is a 5-minute walk from local eateries.

LA49 Hotel

Address: 22//2 Soi Phrom Phak (Thonglor 13 Yak Torsak 1), Klongton-Nua, Vadhana, Bangkok; Wattana, Bangkok.

LA is a 3-minute walk from Samitivej Sukhumvit Hospital.Residence 49 provides lodging with sauna access. WiFi is available for free.

All apartments feature a balcony, air conditioning, and some include a dining room and a sitting space with a satellite flat-screen TV. All apartments also offer a kitchenette with a microwave, toaster, and refrigerator.

The Emporium Shopping Mall is a 15-minute walk away, while Soi Cowboy is 1.8 kilometers distant. Suvarnabhumi Airport is 19 kilometers from LA.Residence 49 provides a complimentary shuttle service to surrounding attractions.

Budget Hotels in Bangkok

Siam Stadium Hostel

Address: 134 Rama 1 Road Wangmai; Pathumwan, Pathumwan, Bangkok..

Situated in Bangkok and just 700 meters away from Jim Thompson House, Siam Stadium Hostel provides a common lounge area, non-smoking rooms, and complimentary WiFi for guests. Nearby attractions include SEA LIFE Bangkok Ocean World, Central World, and Gaysorn Village Shopping Mall. The Central Embassy is 2.5 kilometers distant, while Amarin Plaza is 1.9 kilometers away.

Every room in the hostel has bed linen and towels.

MBK Center, Siam Paragon Mall, and Siam Discovery are all popular places to visit near Siam Stadium Hostel. The closest airport is Don Mueang International Airport, which is 25 kilometers away.

Tini Kati Hostel

Address: 5/10 Soi Silom 3 (Soi Pipat) Silom Rd. Bangrak, Bang Rak, Bangkok

Tini Kati Hostel is a 4-story hotel in Bangkok's Bang Rak area, 200 meters from the colorful Patpong and 900 meters from Lumpini Park. It offers free WiFi throughout the property. Guests may explore the vibrant surrounding neighborhood, which has a variety of shops and eateries. The home is a 10-minute walk from the Sala Daeng BTS sky train station and the Silom MRT subway station.

Each unit has air conditioning and towels for visitors' comfort and offers both private and dormitory rooms. All private rooms have a flat-screen television. Guests residing in dormitory rooms have access to a common restroom. While staying at Tini Kati Hostel, guests may also take use of a communal kitchen, laundry facilities, and complementary all-day snacks, tea, and coffee.

Every morning, Tini Kati Hostel offers a complimentary self-service breakfast.

Only two skytrain stations separate popular retail malls such as Siam Paragon, Central World, and MBK retail Centre. Snake Farm is 2 kilometers away, while the closest airport is Don Mueang International Airport, which is 28 kilometers away from Tini Kati Hostel.

Luk Hostel

Address: 382-384-386 Vanich 1 Road Kwan Chakkrawat Khet Samphanthawong; Bangkok..

Luk Hostel features a common lounge, balcony, restaurant, and bar. The property is around 2.2 kilometers from Wat Saket, 2.7 kilometers from Temple of the Emerald Buddha, and 2.8 kilometers from Wat Pho. The hotel offers evening entertainment and operates a front desk that operates 24 hours a day.

Rooms at the hostel have a common bathroom with a bidet and a hairdryer, as well as free WiFi. Rooms at Luk Hostel include bed linen and towels.

The hotel serves an American or vegetarian breakfast.

The Grand Palace is 3 kilometers away, while Khao San Road is 3.2 kilometers away. Don Mueang International Airport is 27 kilometers from the accommodation.

Mind Day Hostel Khaosan

Address: 214 Chakrabongse Rd.,, Banglamphu, Pranakorn, Bangkok.

Mind Day Hostel Khaosan, located in Bangkok and 500 metres from Khao San Road, offers a common lounge, non-smoking rooms, free WiFi throughout the hotel, and a patio. This 2-star hostel has a common kitchen and baggage storage. The Grand Palace is 1.8 kilometers distant, while Wat Pho is 3.3 kilometers away.

Certain rooms are equipped with a kitchenette containing a refrigerator and a microwave.

Nearby attractions include the Bangkok National Museum, the Temple of the Emerald Buddha, and Wat Saket. Don Mueang International Airport is 26 kilometers away from Mind Day Hostel Khaosan.

Backpack Station

Address: Wattana, Sukhumvit 71 Road 24-24/1 Soi Pridi Banomyong 2; Bangkok

Backpack Station, located in Bangkok and 3.8 kilometers from Emporium Shopping Mall, has a common lounge, non-smoking rooms, free WiFi throughout the hotel, and a patio. The property is around 4.9 kilometers from Queen Sirikit National Convention Centre, 6.7 kilometers from Central Embassy, and 7.1 kilometers from Amarin Plaza. Family rooms are available at the hostel.

Lumpini Park is 7.2 kilometers away, while Gaysorn Village Shopping Mall is 7.3 kilometers distant. Suvarnabhumi Airport is 24 kilometers away from Backpack Station.

Chapter 5

<u>EXPLORING THE CITY</u>

Must Visit Places In Bangkok

1. Grand Palace & Wat Phra Kaew

Visiting Hours: Daily from 8:30 AM to 3:30 PM
Entrance Fee: THB 500
Estimated Duration: Approximately 2 hours

The Grand Palace is undeniably one of the most significant landmarks in Bangkok. Constructed in 1782, it formerly served as the official residence of the Royal Family until 1925. The Grand Palace still holds significant importance as the venue for official royal events and state functions even though the King now resides in Dusit Palace.

This vast complex comprises stunning ornate buildings, pavilions, courtyards, and well-maintained gardens. Among its key structures is Wat Phra Kaew, known as the Temple of the Emerald Buddha, which houses the revered Emerald Buddha, making it the most sacred Buddhist temple in Thailand.

Visitors can explore the Grand Palace on their own or opt for a guided tour to delve deeper into its rich history.

2. Wat Pho

Visiting Hours: Daily from 8 AM to 6:30 PM
Entrance Fee: THB 200
Estimated Duration: Approximately 1 hour

Situated south of the Grand Palace, Wat Pho, or the Temple of the Reclining Buddha, is home to nearly 400 gilded Buddha images, including its spectacular 15-meter-tall and 46-meter-long reclining Buddha statue.

As one of Thailand's six temples of the highest grade, alongside Wat Arun, Wat Pho holds immense significance. The temple holds historical significance as it served as Thailand's inaugural public university and gained renown for being the birthplace of traditional Thai massage, a practice that continues to be taught and practiced within its premises to this day.

Due to its historical importance and proximity to the Grand Palace, guided tours often combine visits to Wat Pho and the Grand Palace.

3. Wat Saket

Visiting Hours: Daily from 7:30 AM to 7 PM
Entrance Fee: THB 100
Estimated Duration: Approximately 1 hour

Wat Saket, also known as the Golden Mount, is an Ayutthaya-era Buddhist temple distinguished by its striking gold chedi.

Perched atop an 80-meter-tall artificial hill, around 2.5 km east of the Grand Palace, Wat Saket rewards visitors with panoramic views of Bangkok after climbing over 300 steps to reach the stupa at its peak.

As no BTS or MRT stations are in close proximity to Wat Saket, visitors can easily reach it via Grab from the Grand Palace or on foot from Wat Suthat. Guided tours are also available.

4. Wat Suthat Thepwararam / Giant Swing

Visiting Hours: Daily from 8:30 AM to 9 PM
Entrance Fee: THB 100
Estimated Duration: Approximately 30 minutes to 1 hour

Situated between the Grand Palace and Wat Saket, Wat Suthat Thepwararam is one of Bangkok's oldest Buddhist temples and holds the status of one of the city's ten royal temples of the first grade.

While Wat Suthat is a noteworthy temple in its own right, the Giant Swing located outside its gates is a unique attraction. Standing at a height of more than 21 meters, the structure comprises two red pillars elegantly linked by a finely carved crossbar. The Giant Swing was once used in a Brahmin thanksgiving ceremony where young men would swing up to 24 meters in the air, trying to grab a bag of silver coins with their teeth. This practice was discontinued in 1932.

A convenient way to visit Wat Suthat Thepwararam and the Giant Swing is by purchasing a Hop-On-Hop-Off pass, which offers set routes to popular tourist attractions across the city, including the Giant Swing.

5. Wat Arun

Visiting Hours: Daily from 8:30 AM to 6 PM
Entrance Fee: THB 100
Estimated Duration: Approximately 30 minutes to 1 hour

Located across the Chao Phraya River from Wat Pho, Wat Arun is not only a prominent temple in Bangkok but also celebrated for its captivating riverside setting and unique architecture.

Easily accessible from Wat Pho, visitors can take a short ferry ride from Tha Thien Pier for THB 4 to reach Wat Arun.

6. Jim Thompson House

Visiting Hours: 9AM-6PM, daily
Entrance Fee: THB 200
Estimated Duration: About 1-2 hrs

Situated in the Siam area, approximately a 10-minute stroll from the MBK Shopping Center, the Jim Thompson House serves as a museum displaying the remarkable Southeast Asian art collection of American businessman Jim Thompson. He is widely credited for reviving Thailand's silk industry during the 1950s and 1960s.

Aside from its captivating exhibits, the Jim Thompson House holds an intriguing mystery surrounding Jim Thompson's own disappearance. In 1967, he vanished while walking in Malaysia's Cameron Highlands, and to this day, his body has never been found, making his disappearance an enigmatic event.

7. Erawan Shrine

Visiting Hours: 6AM-11PM, daily
Entrance Fee: FREE
Estimated Duration: About 15-30 mins

The Erawan Shrine ranks among the most popular Hindu shrines in Bangkok. Throughout the day, visitors will witness worshippers offering flowers, incense sticks, and fruit to the gilded statue of Phra Phrom, the Thai representation of Brahma, the Hindu god of creation.

Located close to the Chit Lom Station of the Skytrain, the Erawan Shrine lies in a bustling commercial area between Siam and Sukhumvit, making it convenient for visitors to stop by while shopping. The shrine also hosts traditional Thai dance performances throughout the day.

8. Erawan Museum

Visiting Hours: 9AM-7PM, daily
Entrance Fee: THB 400
Estimated Duration: About 1-2 hrs

The Erawan Museum stands as one of the most distinctive museums in Bangkok. Its main attraction is a colossal bronze statue of a three-headed elephant, an awe-inspiring structure weighing 250 tons and measuring 29 meters in height and 39 meters in length.

Though it requires a short Grab ride from Samrong Station, the last stop on the Skytrain's Sukhumvit

Line, the unique experience offered by the Erawan Museum makes the journey worthwhile for those seeking something extraordinary in Bangkok.

9. Bangkok Art and Culture Center (BACC)

Visiting Hours: 10AM-9PM, Tue-Sun (closed on Mondays)
Entrance Fee: FREE
Estimated Duration: About 2-3 hrs

The Bangkok Art and Culture Center (BACC) is a contemporary arts hub featuring free exhibitions spread across ten floors. This vibrant space houses commercial art galleries, cafes, bookstores, and craft shops, offering a diverse cultural experience.

Situated near the MBK Shopping Center, BACC can be easily accessed through the National Stadium BTS Station, making it a perfect stop for exploration while shopping in the Siam area.

Fun Things To Do In Bangkok

1. Discover Bangkok's Diverse Markets

Just like its street food, Bangkok is renowned for its vibrant markets. Ranging from food markets to weekend markets, floating markets to night markets, the city boasts an array of market experiences catering to various tastes.

A visit to at least one market is an essential part of the Bangkok experience for any first-time visitor. Some recommended market highlights include Chatuchak Weekend Market, Or Tor Kor Market, and Khlong Lat Mayom Floating Market.

2. Embark on a Food Tour

Bangkok's reputation as a haven for street food is well-deserved. CNN has hailed it as the ultimate street food city, and with good reason. Irrespective of where one looks or the time of day, delectable dishes seem to be waiting at every corner, offering a gastronomic delight.

For a remarkable street food experience, explore the area around Yaowarat Road in Chinatown, which hosts some of the best and most iconic street food stalls in Bangkok.

3. Participate in a Thai Cooking Class

Discovering the local cuisine is an integral part of any trip, and a Thai cooking class provides an engaging way to delve into the flavors and culinary secrets of the region. Similar to a food tour, a cooking class allows participants to gain insight into the intricacies of Thai cuisine, providing an immersive experience in understanding the unique flavors and techniques.

4. Explore Bang Kachao on a Bicycle

For those seeking a respite from the hustle and bustle of Bangkok's urban jungle, a tranquil retreat can be found in Bang Kachao, an artificial island formed by a bend in the Chao Phraya River. Often referred to as Bangkok's "Green Lung," Bang

Kachao spans 16 sq km and is characterized by lush mangrove forests, palm trees, and dense jungle. Here, one can escape the towering skyscrapers and instead immerse themselves in a serene environment of rustic wooden houses and elevated pathways over canals, best explored by bicycle. Bang Kachao serves as an authentic oasis within the bustling city of Bangkok.

To reach Bang Kachao, one can take a longtail boat from Wat Khlong Toey Nok Temple. Once on the island, bicycles are available for rent, providing an excellent means to explore and savor the true beauty of this green sanctuary.

5. Experience Bangkok's Vibrant Nightlife

Bangkok boasts a vibrant nightlife scene, attracting tourists, particularly young backpackers, with its numerous bars and entertainment options. For bar-hopping adventures, Soi 11 in Sukhumvit and Khao San Road are popular destinations. Additionally, the city offers a plethora of captivating rooftop bars, such as Blue Sky on the 24th floor of Centara Grand, providing panoramic views and an unforgettable atmosphere.

6. Indulge in a Relaxing Massage or Spa Treatment

For those seeking relaxation and rejuvenation, a massage or spa treatment is a must-do in Bangkok. Whether opting for a foot massage, body massage, or indulging in a full-blown spa experience, Thailand's renowned hospitality ensures a delightful pampering session. The city is replete with massage parlors and spas, offering a range of treatments, providing visitors with ample options to unwind and destress.

7. Witness an Authentic Muay Thai Kickboxing Match

Combat sports enthusiasts have the opportunity to experience live Muay Thai action at Bangkok's prominent stadiums, Lumpinee and Rajadamnern. Second class seats are often recommended for the best vantage point, as ringside tickets can be too close to the action, making it challenging to fully appreciate the fights.

8. Enjoy a Chao Phraya River Cruise

The Chao Phraya River plays a significant role in Bangkok's landscape, flowing through the heart of the city and serving as a vital mode of transportation for countless commuters daily.

For tourists, a Chao Phraya River cruise offers an excellent opportunity to witness some of Bangkok's iconic attractions, including Wat Arun, Wat Pho, and the Grand Palace.

Day Tours From Bangkok

1. Visit the Maeklong Railway Market

A fascinating experience awaits at the Maeklong Railway Market, located approximately 80 km west of Bangkok in the province of Samut Songkhram. This unique market is set up so close to active train tracks that vendors and buyers must swiftly clear their stalls to make way for passing trains. The sight of vendors hastily packing and moving their goods as the train approaches is an intriguing spectacle, making the trip to Maeklong Railway Market an adventure often combined with a visit to Amphawa Floating Market.

2. Explore the Historic City of Ayutthaya

Founded in 1350, Ayutthaya is a UNESCO World Heritage Site and was once the illustrious capital of Siam. Flourishing between the 14th and 18th centuries, it emerged as one of the world's largest urban areas and a significant hub for global diplomacy and trade.

Tragically, the city fell to the Burmese army in 1767, leading to its destruction, and it was never rebuilt. Today, Ayutthaya's captivating ruins attract countless visitors on day trips from Bangkok, with the iconic Buddha head enshrined within a banyan tree serving as one of its most recognizable landmarks.

3. Enjoy a Day at a Floating Market

With its extensive network of canals and waterways, Bangkok boasts numerous floating markets. For an authentic local experience, Khlong Lat Mayom

Floating Market, just outside Central Bangkok, comes highly recommended. However, if one seeks a grander scale, Amphawa and Damnoen Saduak Floating Markets are renowned for their colorful boats and bustling ambiance, though they can get crowded with tourists.

4. Relax on the Beaches of Pattaya

Pattaya, a captivating resort town nestled along the eastern coast of the Gulf of Thailand, beckons travelers seeking coastal charm and vibrant beach experiences. Located about 150 kilometers to the south of the bustling metropolis of Bangkok. Pattaya stands as an enticing getaway for beach lovers and adventure seekers alike. While Pattaya once carried a reputation as a seedy beach destination, it has undergone a transformation, now catering to families and couples, with its alluring white sand beaches and an array of exciting water sports such as snorkeling, jet skiing, and parasailing.

5. Cross River Kwai Bridge

"The Bridge on the River Kwai," a renowned film released in 1957, depicts the construction of the

Burma Railway during the 1942-1943 period. Also referred to as the "Death Railway," it earned its name due to the immense toll it took on civilian laborers and Allied prisoners, resulting in the tragic loss of over 100,000 lives.

For history enthusiasts, a day tour from Bangkok provides a chance to ride on the Thai-Burma Railway in Kanchanaburi, offering insights into this poignant chapter of World War II.

6. Experience the Seaside Charm of Hua Hin

Nestled less than three hours south of Bangkok, Hua Hin is a picturesque resort town that may not be as well-known but offers a delightful escape. Renowned for being a favored retreat of the late King Bhumibol Adulyadej, Hua Hin boasts an enchanting ambiance. For travelers with limited time, a day tour, bookable through Klook, provides an excellent opportunity to explore the captivating attractions of Hua Hin.

How Many Days Should You Stay in Bangkok?

For first-time visitors to Bangkok, dedicating 3-4 days to explore the city is an ideal duration. This time frame allows ample time to visit major attractions and even venture on a day trip.

If feasible, consider planning your stay over the weekend, as some of the finest markets are closed during weekdays.

Chapter 6

CULTURAL EXPERIENCES IN BANGKOK

Thai Traditional Dance and Music Performances

Thai traditional dance and music performances are captivating displays of the country's rich cultural heritage. The graceful movements and intricate costumes of classical Thai dance, such as the "Khon" and "Ram Thai" dances, tell enchanting stories from ancient Thai literature. Accompanied by traditional music, including the "pi phat" ensemble and "khim" zither, these performances evoke a sense of elegance and charm. Additionally, the vibrant folk dances like "Lakhon Chatri" and "Rong Ngeng" showcase regional traditions and celebrations. Attending these performances is a wonderful way to immerse oneself in the artistic beauty and timeless traditions of Thailand's cultural heritage.

Floating Markets

Floating markets are a unique and iconic aspect of Thailand's cultural heritage. These bustling markets take place on rivers and canals, with vendors selling their wares from traditional wooden boats. Visitors can experience the charm of buying fresh fruits, vegetables, snacks, and local handicrafts directly from the boats. Damnoen Saduak Floating Market and Amphawa Floating Market are among the most popular ones near Bangkok. Tourists can enjoy boat rides, sample delicious street food, and witness the vibrant atmosphere filled with colors and scents. Floating markets offer an authentic glimpse into traditional Thai life and commerce, making them a must-visit attraction for travelers seeking a delightful and immersive experience.

Thai Cooking Classes

Thai cooking classes provide a hands-on experience for travelers interested in mastering the art of Thai cuisine. These classes offer an opportunity to learn from experienced chefs and explore the intricate flavors of Thai dishes. Participants get to prepare popular dishes like Pad Thai, Tom Yum Goong, and Green Curry. Many classes begin with a visit to local markets to purchase fresh ingredients, enhancing the understanding of Thai culinary culture. Whether it's a half-day course or a full-fledged culinary adventure, Thai cooking classes leave visitors with valuable cooking skills and lasting memories of authentic Thai flavors to recreate at home.

Traditional Thai Massage and Spa Treatments

Renowned worldwide, traditional Thai massage and spa treatments offer a rejuvenating experience to unwind and pamper the body and mind. Based on ancient healing practices, Thai massage involves stretching, acupressure, and rhythmic compressions to promote relaxation and balance energy flow. Spa treatments combine traditional Thai herbs, essential oils, and skilled techniques to provide a holistic approach to well-being. Whether in luxury spas or affordable wellness centers, indulging in traditional Thai massage or spa treatments is an essential part of the Thailand experience. It offers a chance to soothe tired muscles, alleviate stress, and revel in the age-old art of healing practiced for generations.

Chapter 7

THAI LANGUAGE AND COMMUNICATION GUIDE

Useful Phrases You'll Need in Thailand

Mastering some useful Thai phrases can significantly enrich your travel experience in Thailand, demonstrating genuine regard for the local culture and facilitating more effective communication with the residents.

Greetings in Thai

It's crucial to remember that each of the phrases below requires adding a gender marker at the end. If you are female, conclude your sentence with "Ka" (khaa), and if you are male, use "Krup" (khrap).

1. Hello - Sa Wat Dee (sa-wat-dee)

Greet everyone you encounter along your journey. Although you might stumble over the word initially, Thais will gladly assist with pronunciation, and this simple greeting will undoubtedly enhance your visit.

2. Thank You - Kawp Koon (kop-koon)

Exhibiting politeness can greatly enhance your experience. If possible, try to perform the "wai" [deep bow] when expressing gratitude.

3. Yes | No - Chai | Mai Chai (chai / my-chai)

Learning the basics is always a wise move. Notwithstanding your complete understanding of the language, you'll find that a straightforward "chai" (yes) or "mai chai" (no) is often sufficient for effective communication.

4. I Don't Understand - Mai Khao Jai (my-cow-jai)

Don't get frustrated when faced with something you don't understand. Instead, repeat this phrase until someone can (hopefully) translate.

5. Excuse Me - Kor Tot (kor-tot)

Thailand can be crowded, whether you're riding the sky train or hopping between islands by boat. Be prepared for these situations and learn how to say "excuse me."

6. Goodbye - Lah Gorn (la-gon)

When parting ways and uncertain about what to say, a simple "lah gorn" and/or a "wai" will suffice.

Asking for Directions

7. Turn Left | Turn Right - Leo Sai | Leo Kwaa (lee-yo-sigh|lee-yo-kwa)

Avoid being taken advantage of by taxi drivers. Equip yourself with a map and the ability to give basic directions in Thai, reducing the chances of arriving at the wrong destination.

8. Where Is The Bathroom? - Haawng Naam Yuu Thee Nai?? (hong-nam-you-tee-nye))

Bathrooms can be scarce in Thailand, and sometimes you won't find one until it's almost too late. Spare yourself the frantic search with this straightforward phrase (and be prepared for squat toilets and bum guns).

9. Stop | Go - Yut | Bai (yut | bye)

Impress your driver with these directional essentials to navigate with ease. Mastering the skill of giving directions to a taxi, tuk-tuk, or Songtaew driver will undoubtedly prove beneficial in terms of both saving time and money during your travels.

10. Slow Down - Hai Chah Long (high-cha-lom)

This phrase comes in handy when your tuk-tuk driver is speeding, and you'd like them to slow down. Alternatively, it can be useful when giving directions to someone.

At The Bar/Restaurants

11. No Sugar - Mai Sai Nam Tam ((my-sigh-nam-tam)|

What salt is to the western world, that is what Sugar is to Thailand. It finds its way into everything from noodle soup to black coffee. If you prefer your coffee less sweet or want to avoid the extra calories, know this simple phrase.

12. I'm Hungry - Hiu (hee-yoo)

Thailand boasts some of the most delectable dishes globally. Learn how to express your hunger without resorting to gestures like rubbing your stomach.

13. I Like It A Little Bit Spicy - Pet Noi (chop-pet-noy)

Spicy food is adored by Thai locals, and certain eateries deliberately create mildly spicy dishes, recognizing that foreigners might not have a high tolerance for heat. To avoid overwhelming your taste buds, acquaint yourself with this practical phrase.

Water - Nam (nam)
This is one of the most crucial words to learn in the Thai language, especially when exploring under the scorching heat of the day and feeling dehydrated.

Delicious - Aroi (a-roy)

To express appreciation for the delightful food you just savored, a heartfelt compliment to the cook will surely earn you a warm smile in return.

At The Market

How Much Is This? - A Nee Tao Rai? (a-nee-tow-rye)

While Thais are incredibly friendly, as with any other place, travelers should stay alert for potential scams. Asking "how much" in the local language helps avoid overpaying for the same item compared to locals.

Too Expensive - Phaeng Mark Pai (feng-mak-pie)

If someone is charging you more than reasonable for souvenirs, don't hesitate to speak up with this marketplace phrase.

Numbers in Thai

Learning Thai numbers is essential for everyday interactions, whether it's shopping, taking public transportation, or understanding prices. These are the numbers from one to ten in Thai:

1. หนึ่ง (nèung)
2. สอง (săawng)
3. สาม (săam)

4. สี่ (sìi)
5. ห้า (hâa)
6. หก (hòk)
7. เจ็ด (jèt)
8. แปด (bpàet)
9. เก้า (gâo)
10. สิบ (sìp)

To form numbers beyond ten, combine the word for the tens place with the unit number. For example:

11. สิบเอ็ด (sìp èt) - Ten one
12. สิบสอง (sìp sǎawng) - Ten two
20. ยี่สิบ (yîi sìp) - Two ten
21. ยี่สิบเอ็ด (yîi sìp èt) - Two ten one
30. สามสิบ (sǎam sìp) - Three ten
100. หนึ่งร้อย (nèung rói) - One hundred

Remember that Thai numbers may have slight variations in pronunciation depending on the region, so practice with locals to improve your understanding and pronunciation of Thai numbers.

Making Friends

Have You Eaten Yet? - Gin Khao Lou Mai? (gin-cow-lou-mye)

Beyond its literal meaning, in Thailand, this phrase takes on a deeper significance. It serves not only as a simple "hello" but also as a conversation starter and a genuine way to check in on someone's well-being.

Very Beautiful | Handsome - Suay | Lo Mak (soo-way | low-mak)

A sincere compliment holds tremendous power, especially when traveling in a foreign land.

For Everything Else

I Am Very Hot - Ron Mak (ron -mak)
With scorching temperatures during the hot season, this phrase comes in handy to interact with locals or explain the need for assistance when you're red, sweating, and in need of relief.

No Problem - Mai Bpen Rai [my-pen-rye]

Missed a flight? Mai bpen rai. Food poisoning taking its toll? Mai bpen rai. Thais dislike losing face, so embracing a positive attitude in challenging situations fosters a better connection with locals.

Chapter 8

WHAT AND WHERE TO EAT IN BANGKOK

Thai food boasts must-try dishes for every food enthusiast, bursting with exotic flavors, vibrant colors, and the perfect balance of sweet, sour, spicy, and salty tastes, truly capturing Thailand's essence.

Right from the iconic Pad Thai down to the aromatic Tom Yum Goong, and from the tasty Green Curry to the refreshing Som Tam, The diverse selection of delectable dishes in Thai cuisine will take your taste buds on a journey to the vibrant streets of Bangkok. Embark on a gastronomic adventure as we explore the world of must-try Thai foods, leaving you yearning for more culinary delights.

Must-Try Thai Dishes

1. Pad Thai
Commencing with a timeless classic, Pad Thai showcases stir-fried rice noodles tossed with shrimp, tofu, bean sprouts, eggs, and a tangy tamarind-based sauce. Adorned with crushed peanuts and fresh lime, this dish artfully balances flavors and textures.

2. Tom Yum Goong

Exemplifying bold and refreshing Thai flavors, Tom Yum Goong is a hot and sour shrimp soup infused with lemongrass, galangal, lime leaves, and chilies. Bursting with succulent shrimp and mushrooms, this soup delivers a delightful explosion of taste.

3. Green Curry

A creamy and aromatic delight, Thai green curry combines a paste of green chilies, garlic, lemongrass, and fragrant spices. Simmered in coconut milk, tender meat or vegetables create a luscious curry, perfect with steamed jasmine rice.

4. Som Tam

Refreshingly zesty, Som Tam, or green papaya salad, harmonizes shredded green papaya with tomatoes, green beans, peanuts, and a tangy dressing of lime juice, fish sauce, garlic, and chili, offering a vibrant mix of crunch and spice.

5. Massaman Curry

A unique Thai dish influenced by Indian and Muslim flavors, Massaman curry delights with slow-cooked meat, potatoes, onions, and roasted peanuts in a rich, fragrant, and mildly spiced curry.

6. Pad Kra Pao

Uncomplicated yet incredibly flavorful, Pad Kra Pao features minced chicken or pork stir-fried with garlic, chilies, and holy basil leaves, served over steamed rice with a fried egg, a popular choice for both locals and visitors.

7. Mango Sticky Rice

Indulge in a delightful dessert with Mango Sticky Rice, blending ripe mangoes' natural sweetness with sticky glutinous rice drizzled with coconut cream, a heavenly combination of flavors and textures.

8. Khao Soi

A comforting and aromatic noodle soup hailing from Northern Thailand, Khao Soi features egg noodles in a rich curry broth, topped with tender braised meat, crispy noodles, and pickled mustard greens, creating a culinary delight.

The Characteristics of Thai Foods

Thai cuisine's renown lies in its bold flavors, aromatic herbs, and vibrant colors, skillfully balancing sweet, sour, spicy, and salty tastes. Lime juice, tamarind, fish sauce, chili peppers, and palm sugar create a complex flavor profile that captivates the palate. Thai cooking incorporates fresh and aromatic herbs like lemongrass, kaffir lime leaves, galangal, and Thai basil, elevating dishes with distinctive fragrances and tastes. The cuisine's fiery spiciness, achieved through the use of chili peppers, distinguishes Thai food, adding an exhilarating kick. Thai cuisine embraces a diverse array of ingredients, from vegetables and herbs to meat, seafood, and tropical fruits, celebrating the natural bounty of the land. The textural pleasures vary, encompassing crispiness found in deep-fried dishes, tenderness in braised meats, and the refreshing crunch of fresh vegetables. Aesthetic presentation and harmony in all aspects of the meal reflect Thai values, creating a feast for both the senses and the eyes.

Street Food Culture

Thailand's vibrant street food culture is an integral part of its culinary tapestry. The bustling street markets buzz with tantalizing grills, sizzling woks, and mouthwatering snacks. Street vendors present an array of dishes, inviting locals and tourists alike to savor authentic Thai flavors in a lively and casual setting.

Popular Street Food Spots in Bangkok

Bangkok, synonymous with street food, offers an unforgettable experience for food lovers. Amidst bright pink taxis, modern shopping malls, and motorbike racers, certain areas stand out as havens for delectable street food.

1. Yaowarat Road (Chinatown):
 Yaowarat Road in Bangkok's Chinatown lures with delightful Chinese and Thai street food. Stalls offer dishes like Hainanese chicken rice, dim sum, crispy pork, and flavorful seafood delights.

2. Khao San Road:
Vibrant Khao San Road boasts lively nightlife and a variety of street food, including Pad Thai, mango sticky rice, grilled satay, and exotic fried insects.

3. Or Tor Kor Market:
A top fresh market, Or Tor Kor Market tempts with Thai curries, tropical fruits, grilled seafood, and appetizing snacks like fish cakes and spring rolls.

4. Chatuchak Weekend Market:

The expansive Chatuchak Weekend Market is not only one of the world's largest markets but also a treasure trove of street food. Visitors can enjoy coconut ice cream, grilled sausages, Thai iced tea, and grilled seafood.

5. Victory Monument:
The bustling Victory Monument area is home to numerous street food vendors offering a blend of Thai and international delicacies. Don't miss the famed boat noodle alley with its rich beef or pork noodles.

6. Soi Rambuttri:
Adjacent to Khao San Road, Soi Rambuttri offers a quieter setting to savor delicious street food, featuring stir-fried noodles, fruit shakes, and grilled skewers.

7. Banglamphu Market:
Banglamphu Market in the lively Banglamphu area presents a plethora of street food options, including traditional Thai dishes, refreshing tropical fruit shakes, and grilled seafood.

These popular street food spots in Bangkok are just a taste of the diverse culinary adventure that awaits. With vendors and stalls lining the city's streets, Bangkok truly stands as a haven for food enthusiasts from all over the world. Exploring the rich and tantalizing street food scene is an essential part of any visit to this vibrant city.

Bangkok Street Food Tip: *In Bangkok, Mondays are dedicated to citywide street cleaning, leading many street food cart vendors to enjoy a day off. Expect about a 50% decrease in street food availability on Mondays. While some vendors may still be open, it's best not to solely rely on street food on Mondays.*

BEST RESTAURANTS TO EAT IN BANGKOK

Bangkok boasts an incredible food scene, and some of our favorite restaurants include:

1. Rongros

Situated along the Chao Phraya River, Rongros offers not only delicious but also affordable Thai cuisine. The restaurant's view of Wat Arun, especially at night, adds to the dining experience, making it a must-visit for those seeking excellent yet budget-friendly Thai food in Bangkok.

2. Sanguan Sri
A Michelin-recommended restaurant since 1970, Sanguan Sri serves some of the best Thai curry, a true delight for any food lover exploring Bangkok's culinary offerings.

3. Somsak Pu Ob
While Jay Fai has gained fame, Somsak Pu Ob is another legendary Bangkok street food stall worth knowing. They serve delectable pots of glass noodles with prawn or crab, a true gem for street food enthusiasts.

4. Wattana Panich
Wattana Panich boasts a giant cauldron of beef stew simmering for over forty years, a unique find that guarantees a memorable dining experience in Bangkok.

5. Kim Nguan Fish Ball Chom Thong
This Michelin-recommended restaurant may be off the beaten path, but their fish ball noodle soups are a

treat for those with a penchant for this delightful dish.

Bangkok's culinary wonders extend beyond street food, and these restaurants are a testament to the city's gastronomic diversity. Whether exploring vibrant markets or seeking unique dining experiences, Bangkok never fails to tantalize the taste buds.

Chapter 9

SHOPPING IN BANGKOK

Although I usually avoid extensive shopping during my travels, Bangkok is an exception. The variety of styles, latest fashion, and dirt-cheap prices make shopping in Bangkok irresistible. It's even cheaper than India, so I recommend bringing an empty suitcase to this shopaholic's paradise.

Where to Shop in Bangkok Irrespective of Budget

Bangkok offers a plethora of malls, street shops, and markets, making it a shopper's haven. To simplify your shopping experience, I've compiled this Bangkok shopping guide based on my visits to this metropolis.

Budget Shopping Centers in Bangkok

As a thrifty shopper, I adore budget wholesale malls and the array of street markets in Bangkok. If you share my passion for budget-friendly shopping or seek the best street shopping spots, read on for helpful tips.

Here are some of my favorite locations to shop on a tight budget in Bangkok:

1. Platinum Shopping Center

Among all the shopping options in Bangkok, this is my ultimate choice for affordable shopping. Whenever I visit the city, I ensure to spend a few hours there without fail. Shoes, accessories, women's/men's apparel, and handicrafts all have their own sections and floors at Platinum.

Platinum Mall is still my favorite place to shop for clothes in Bangkok.

2. Market in Pratunam

This lively Bangkok retail market is directly across from Platinum Mall, with throngs of sellers selling wholesale clothes, shoes, and accessories all day. This is one of the better street shopping possibilities, but be cautious with your money in Bangkok because pick pocketing is rampant.

From Petchaburi Road to Baiyoke Towers, Pratunam extends, offering plenty of opportunities for budget-friendly shopping. The shops are open until 2100 hours, but then the night market opens with a different selection. Both the day and night markets are worth visiting.

3. Square Indra

Indra Square is very adjacent to Pratunam, and the only significant difference between the two is that there is another mall where you may shop within, under air conditioning, if it gets too hot outside. While the prices may be slightly higher compared to the Pratunam street shops outside, there is less room for negotiation. However, the clothes, bags, and accessories are still incredibly affordable.

4. Bangkapi Mall and its Adjacent Markets

In a large indoor mall, Bangkapi Mall offers a wide choice of clothing, accessories, and shoes. Along with restaurants and opulent leisure areas. Although the mall contains branded showrooms, you can still discover inexpensive and fantastic discounts on occasion. The greatest part, though, are the outside stores in an open area called the Tavanna market. Outside, you'd likely find greater deals and more variety.

5. Electronics Plaza Pantip

If you're looking for heavily discounted electronics, this is the place to go. This IT mall is a 2-minute walk from Platinum Fashion Mall. You can literally buy anything to satiate your geeky desires here. Pantip is 'the' location to buy electronics, from computers to the latest phones, cameras, MP3 players, printers, games, and all kinds of hardware and software.

Even retailers from other regions of the country travel to Pantip to get a good deal and take out the middleman. There are numerous shops to select from, which can be daunting at first. I would recommend spending some time comparing prices and retailers in order to find the finest deal electronics.

Bangkok's Mid-Range Shopping Malls

Bangkok's mid-range malls are great, with more designs and higher quality than wholesale malls. You also get more room because the lanes are broader and less crowded. Everyone needs lunch after a long day of shopping, and there are many excellent restaurants, cafes, and vegan Bangkok eateries to pick from.

1. MBK Shopping Mall

The most popular mid-range alternative for both tourists and locals is MBK shopping center. It easily tops the list of the best malls in Bangkok. This mall provides all you need to know about what to buy in Bangkok for ladies.

With over 2000 businesses to pick from and a few cheap stalls, it attracts a large number of shoppers looking for low-cost items without having to rummage through tight lanes. It is a shopaholic's dream, with 8 massive storeys.

This shopping center contains everything from clothing to gadgets, as well as a food court and a supermarket. In contrast to wholesale malls, you get everything under one air-conditioned roof. It's no surprise that customers flock in droves to MBK Center every day.

2. Terminal 21

Terminal 21 is on my list because of its uniqueness. Each floor is created with various city markets across the world in mind. Consequently, every floor showcases a unique city theme, featuring Paris, Rome, the Caribbean, Tokyo, London, Istanbul, and San Francisco, each with its own distinct ambiance. The toilet interiors are also designed with the floor concept in mind. It is worth a visit and highly recommended as one of the high-end malls.

3. The Central World

Central World Plaza is one of the larger malls. For your shopping pleasure, you have two main department stores with over 500 stores to pick from. The prices are unquestionably more than those of MBK, but the quality is significantly outstanding. Furthermore, if you go to the rear of department shops, you will often find sales at throwaway rates (when they just have a few items of a style remaining).

Bangkok's luxury shopping malls

The number of luxury shopping complexes in Bangkok is growing in response to people's desire for more places to shop and dine. Today, there are not one, but five luxury retail centers dotted across Bangkok CBD. If you plan to acquire a condominium in Thailand, keep in mind the location's proximity to luxury malls to optimize your revenue. Here's a list of them in case you're seeking somewhere to satisfy your buying desires.

1 Siam Center and Siam Paragon

Another well-known Bangkok retail area is Siam Paragon. It is home to a variety of high-end fashion labels from throughout the world. It is among the most extensive upscale shopping centers in Southeast Asia, boasting top-notch restaurants, exclusive retail boutiques, and a 16-screen Cineplex. You can simply cross from Siam Paragon to Siam Center and Siam Square One. This is directly across from the Siam BTS Skytrain Station.

2. Icon Siam

Icon Siam is a luxury shopping center on the riverbank in Bangkok.

Icon Siam is a well-known luxury shopping center on the riverfront. Locals refer to this as "the mother of all malls" because it houses over 500 businesses and 100 restaurants from over 30 different countries. Icon Siam was created by the same people who created EmQuarter and Siam Paragon. High-end goods are available here, and a section of the mall houses the Siam Takashimaya, a branch of the 180-year-old Japanese mall Takashimaya Group. The free shuttle boat from Saphan Taksin BTS Station to IconSiam provides a pleasant cruise along the Chao Phrayah river.

Bangkok's Emquarter upscale shopping center
Emquarter has a combined indoor and outdoor space of around 600,000 SQM in Phrom Phong, Bangkok. It is one of the area's major luxury shopping malls and is undoubtedly a destination for those seeking a luxurious shopping experience. Designer brands, well-known restaurants, event spaces, and workplaces may all be found here.

3. 8 Thonglor

Eight Thonglor is a traditional neighborhood in the center of Thonglor. The place is situated only a short distance from Sukhumvit Road and the Thong Lo BTS Station, spanning just a few hundred meters. There are various shops here that specialize in food, beauty, lifestyle, fashion, and wellness.

4. Emporium

Emporium, located opposite the EmQuarter, has been in operation since 1997. The Emporium Gourmet Market, which features the best of Thailand, is one of the mall's most noteworthy features. This supermarket stocks imported fruits and vegetables, meat, and other grocery items. Emporium is connected to Phrom Phong BTS Skytrain Station and Chatrium-powered 5-star Emporium Suites. Famous brands such as Louis Vuitton, Chanel, Cartier, Mont Blanc, and Prada can be found within the mall.

Finally, Bangkok's luxury retail centers provide visitors and locals with a one-of-a-kind and elite shopping experience. These shopping centers feature a wide range of international luxury brands, as well as renowned restaurants, movies, and entertainment. The location of luxury shopping centers is an important feature to consider when buying a condo in Bangkok for real estate investors because it can boost the property's value. Ultimately, Bangkok's upscale shopping centers stand as a valuable asset to the city, offering an exceptional choice for those in search of a luxurious shopping experience right within the urban confines.

Bazaars and local markets in Bangkok

Bangkok's local markets and bazaars are a vital aspect of the city's culture, providing both locals and tourists with an immersive and vibrant shopping experience. These bustling markets offer an insight into the true Thai way of life, displaying a diverse range of things ranging from fresh vegetables and traditional crafts to fashionable fashion items and one-of-a-kind souvenirs. Let us explore further into Bangkok's wonderful world of local markets and bazaars:

1. Local Market Diversity: Bangkok has a varied selection of local marketplaces catering to various interests and tastes. From vast weekend markets like Thailand's largest, Chatuchak Market, to smaller local markets like Talad Rot Fai Ratchada, each market has its own unique charm and specialty.

2. Chatuchak Market (JJ Market): Chatuchak Market is a must-see for shopaholics and an iconic landmark in Bangkok. This vast market offers an unequaled variety of things, including clothing, accessories, home decor, antiques, pets, plants, and much more, with over 8,000 vendors distributed across 27 sections. Visitors can easily spend hours wandering the labyrinthine lanes, eating great street cuisine, and shopping for one-of-a-kind items.

3. Floating Markets: Damnoen Saduak and Amphawa floating markets in Bangkok provide a traditional shopping experience, with sellers selling their items from boats along gorgeous canals. These markets are well-known for their fresh fruits and vegetables, as well as local delicacies, making them ideal for trying Thai food.

4. Night Markets: As the sun sets, Bangkok's night markets come alive, giving a vibrant ambiance with colorful lights, live music, and a diverse assortment of merchandise. The Talad Rod Fai Srinakarin and Talad Rot Fai Ratchada night markets are well-known for their antique and retro products, fashionable apparel, and offbeat finds.

5. Local Crafts and Artisanal Products: For real Thai crafts and artisanal products, visit Pratunam Market, Pak Khlong Talat (the Flower Market), and Khlong Thom Market. Handmade goods, textiles, jewelry, and souvenirs are on display at these markets, reflecting Thailand's rich cultural past.

6. Food Markets and Street Food: Bangkok's food markets and street food booths are a foodie's heaven. Talad Neon Night Market and Or Tor Kor Market are great places to try a variety of exquisite Thai meals, fruits, and desserts.

7. area Markets: Each Bangkok area has its own local market where locals can shop for their daily necessities. Visiting these markets allows you to feel the essence of community life and interact with friendly residents.

8. Bargaining and haggling: Bargaining is a typical practice in many Bangkok neighborhood marketplaces. Visitors can try their negotiating abilities and potentially find amazing prices on a variety of things ranging from apparel to handicrafts.

9. Cultural Experiences: In addition to shopping, Bangkok's local markets and bazaars provide cultural experiences that allow visitors to immerse themselves in Thai culture. Seeing traditional performances, like Thai puppetry or folk music, gives an authentic touch to the shopping experience.

10. Sustainability and Eco-friendly Markets: Eco-friendly markets have grown in popularity in Bangkok in recent years, emphasizing sustainable practices and locally sourced items. These markets are ideal for conscientious consumers who want to support ethical enterprises.

Finally, seeing Bangkok's local markets and bazaars is a fascinating and enlightening experience that provides a more in-depth understanding of Thai culture and lifestyle. These markets are a crucial component of any Bangkok itinerary, from shopping for unique items and relishing excellent street food to socializing with friendly merchants and experiencing cultural performances. Bangkok's local markets are likely to leave you with unforgettable experiences and beloved keepsakes, whether you're a seasoned shopper or an inquisitive traveler.

Shopping Etiquettes to Observe

To have a nice and courteous shopping experience in Bangkok, some shopping etiquette must be followed. Here are some pointers to remember:

1. Smile and greet: Begin your shopping experience with a polite greeting and a smile. Politeness and a friendly manner go a long way in building a positive contact with vendors in Thai society.

2. Polite Bargaining: Bargaining is widespread in Bangkok's markets and smaller shops. Remember to bargain softly and with a friendly demeanor. During negotiations, avoid being overly forceful or hostile.

4. Removing Shoes: You may be forced to remove your shoes before entering some shops or establishments. Look for shoe racks or follow the example of others to determine when to remove your shoes.

5. Avoid pointing with your feet or moving anything with your feet, as feet are considered the lowest part of the body in Thai culture.

6. Merchandise Handling: Use caution when handling merchandise, especially delicate or fragile items. If you want to try on clothing or accessories, always ask permission first.

7. Using Both Hands to Present Money or Credit Cards: When paying for your products, use both hands to present money or credit cards to the vendor. This gesture is considered courteous and shows respect.

8. Accepting Change: When accepting change, use both hands, as this is considered a respectful gesture in Thai culture.

9. Photography: Always obtain permission before photographing merchants or their merchandise. Some vendors may have photographic restrictions.

10. While English is widely spoken in tourist areas, practicing a few basic Thai phrases, such as "hello"

and "thank you," demonstrates appreciation for the local culture.

11. Knowing When to quit Bargaining: Know when to quit bargaining. While it is encouraged to get a good deal, pushing for unreasonable prices can be insulting to merchants.

12. Personal Space: When wandering through crowded markets, keep your personal space in mind. During hectic periods, avoid pushing or shoving and remain patient.

Chapter 10

NIGHTLIFE AND ENTERTAINMENT

Bangkok's nightlife culture is bustling and interesting, with everything from sophisticated rooftop bars to distinctive cocktail bars, lively clubs, and more. The nightlife in Bangkok is as vibrant and diverse as the city itself, and most visitors should plan on taking advantage of the city's attractions. Visitors will want to plan their nightlife adventures with so much to choose from, and this section can help them determine which locations, bars, clubs, and activities to visit when they visit the city.

Bangkok's Best Nightlife Districts

Bangkok has numerous wonderful nightlife places to select from, each offering something unique to visitors. Here are some of Bangkok's most popular nightlife locations.

1. The Khao San Road

Khao San Road, located in central Bangkok, is famed for catering to backpackers and is a refuge for travelers in the area. Visitors looking for loud, entertaining pubs and restaurants as well as budget-friendly options might like this region.

What is the best way to get there?

Take the BTS Skytrain to Saphan Taksin. Take a Chao Phraya Express Boat upriver (boats with a blue or orange flag) from Sathorn Central Pier, which is located adjacent to the BTS station. Exit at Phra Arthit Pier. Khao San Road is about 11 minutes southeast of the dock.

2. The Sukhumvit Road

Sukhumvit Road is well-known for having some of Bangkok's top nightlife options. Sukhumvit Road is a popular place for travelers to come since it has trendy bars, great shopping, and plenty of fancy restaurants and nightclubs. Sukhumvit Road is also home to several well-known nightlife zones and is one of the world's longest boulevards.

What is the best way to get there?

The Bangkok BTS Sukhumvit Line runs alongside the road, therefore travelers can reach this neighborhood by Skytrain. There are numerous BTS stations in this district, but the most popular among visitors are Nana BTS Station, Asok BTS Station, Thong Lo BTS Station, and Ekkamai BTS Station. Asok BTS Station is located in the heart of Sukhumvit Road, therefore passengers looking for a central location should disembark here.

Sukhumvit Road's Famous Nightlife Districts

While there are numerous nightlife alternatives on and near Sukhumvit Road, these are some of the most well-known areas that provide a taste of the many entertainment options available in this sector.

1. Thong Lo

Thong Lo is well-known for its stylish nightlife culture, making it an excellent destination for travelers interested in cocktail bars, boutique shopping, and upscale clubs. This neighborhood attracts both locals and expats, so travelers want to interact should spend the night on Thong Lo, which is located northeast of Thong Lo BTS Station on the Sukhumvit Line.

2. Ekkamai Road

Ekkamai Road, commonly known as Soi Sukhumvit 63, is a popular hangout for locals and foreigners alike. It is home to hipsters, cafés, and delicious restaurants. Ekkamai can be a terrific site to explore if travelers want to experience Bangkok's nightlife outside of the regular tourist spots, and it is also a great spot for foodies looking for distinctive Bangkok specialties and a decent pint of beer. Ekkamai Road lies on the north side of the Sukhumvit Line's Ekkamai BTS Station.

3. Nana

Nana District is an excellent place to visit if you want to sample some racy bars. There are many fantastic places to see in this region, which is well-known for its themed go-go bars. Because Nana Plaza is not as family-friendly as other sites in Bangkok, it is best visited by adults. The Nana Plaza's dazzling neon signs greet visitors as they pass through this vibrant and dynamic region. Nana Plaza is on the Sukhumvit Line, southwest of Nana BTS Station.

4. Asok Soi Cowboy

Soi Cowboy is a popular tourist and expat attraction in Bangkok, featuring around 40 go-go bars. Soi Cowboy is also one of Bangkok's most well-known red-light districts, so daring visitors seeking bright lights and racy sights should visit. Soi Cowboy is a street just northeast of Asok BTS Station.

RCA

RCA, also known as Royal City Avenue, is one of Bangkok's most well-known entertainment districts. This area is a terrific alternative for travelers searching for a range of entertainment options in one location, with amazing clubs, bars, and live music selections. Younger folks tend to attend RCA, which is home to numerous contemporary entertainment establishments. Take the BTS to Phrom Phong or Asok BTS Stations. Visitors should rent a cab from either of these locations and have the driver transport them to RCA.

Silom

Silom, Bangkok's business neighborhood, also boasts a fantastic selection of restaurants and is home to the city's famous Patpong entertainment district, one of the top Bangkok nightlife destinations. While Silom is all business during the day, it comes alive at night with people, pubs, and clubs. This area can get very crowded, so plan accordingly. Si Lom MRT Station is the area's most central MRT stop. Visitors can also use the BTS to the Silom Line's Sala Daeng BTS Station.

Best Bars in Bangkok

Bangkok has so many wonderful bars to pick from, from high-end places to budget dives, that travelers are likely to find something that suits their tastes. Bangkok is a terrific destination for travellers who enjoy drinking and partying, and here are some of the greatest rooftop and traditional bars in the city.

Bangkok's 5 Best Rooftop Bars

Bangkok is famed for its outstanding rooftop bars, and visiting one while in the city can be an unforgettable experience. Visitors may see the Bangkok skyline while sipping cocktails and relaxing high above the city. Those hoping for a truly unique experience can book a reservation at one of Bangkok's rooftop bars after nightfall. With so many amazing bars to pick from, here are some recommendations for the best rooftop bar nightlife in Bangkok.

1. Sala Rattanakosin Rooftop Bar

The Rooftop bar of Sala Rattanakosin Bangkok hotel offers beautiful views of Wat Arun (the Temple of Dawn) and the Chao Phraya River and serves beer, wine, cocktails, and light snacks. Reservations are strongly advised.

2. Rooftop Speakeasy Bar

The Speakeasy Rooftop Bar is located on the 24th and 25th floors of Hotel Muse Bangkok Langsuan - MGallery Collection and offers panoramic city views. The Speakeasy Rooftop Bar, which has a beautiful rooftop sky garden, serves Asian-fusion meals and specializes in exquisite cocktails. Visitors should secure a seat early if they plan on visiting this bar because it is popular and recognized for attracting an affluent clientele.

3. 1826 Rooftop Bar & Mixology Studio

1826 Mixology & Rooftop Bar is a terrific choice for high-end drinks, with amazing sunset views and tasty cocktails prepared from fresh, house-made ingredients, all set in a lovely open-air environment.

The Rembrandt Hotel Suites and Towers' 26th floor bar also provides small plates of Mexican, Indian, and Italian cuisine.

4. Octave

Octave rooftop lounge and bar is located on the 45th floor of Bangkok Marriott Hotel Sukhumvit. With fantastic views and easy access from Sukhumvit Road, this three-level bar is a great location to rest, relax, and enjoy the view. However, if guests are looking forward to partying, they should avoid the first level, which is usually utilized for dining and resting, and instead explore the second or third levels to experience the party scene. Before departing, visitors should take in the open air and panoramic views of the third floor.

5. Above Eleven

Above Eleven is a three-story rooftop bar noted for being a less expensive choice for travelers who want to stop at a rooftop bar but don't want to pay excessive fees. Above Eleven provides Peruvian/Japanese food and an unusual décor made to look like a city park, as well as a selection of distinctive cocktails and a great perspective of downtown Bangkok.

Other Best Bars

Bangkok is ideal for folks who enjoy bar hopping because there are various areas with numerous bars within walking distance of one another. Bangkok's nightlife options also include a wonderful array of pubs catering to a more affluent crowd for more sophisticated travelers. Here are some of the top bars in Bangkok, ranging from ritzy to more casual venues.

<u>The Rabbit Hole</u>

Enjoy the nightlife in Bangkok at this cocktail bar, which has a terrific ambiance, gorgeous multilevel vintage décor, and an almost secret entry (search for the unmarked entrance between Soi 5 and Soi 7). The bar welcomes customers to recline into a comfy chair and order a drink, with open facing cupboards displaying their huge alcohol selection. On Fridays and Saturdays, visitors may enjoy live DJs and should consider booking a reservation ahead of time.

The Bamboo bar

Jazz fans will undoubtedly like The Bamboo Bar. The Bamboo Bar developed a name for itself as a jazz bar with its magnificent décor and live music, and its reputation has only increased over the years owing to the quality of its location. Visitors may enjoy award-winning cocktails while listening to live music. Except on Sundays, live music is performed every day at 9 p.m. The Bamboo Bar is situated on the Chao Phraya River, and there is a dress code in effect after 6:30 p.m.: ladies are encouraged to wear exquisite apparel, while males are asked to wear long trousers and closed-toe shoes.

Smalls

This late-night cocktail bar with a distinct ambience is a perfect place to unwind after a long day of touring. Smalls is decorated in a Parisian style, with low lighting and delicate jazz music playing throughout. This three-story institution has a welcoming lobby as well as an upper space where guests may have a beverage on the terrace. French cuisine is also available, so customers may enjoy a range of culinary items while relaxing with their beverages.

Saxophone

Visitors interested in live jazz and blues concerts may stop by Saxophone. This popular pub spot has a full bar and live entertainment till late at night. Saxophone, which also has a superb restaurant, is the ideal location for visitors to get a meal and a drink before settling down for the evening.

Bangkok's Best Nightclubs and Dance Venues

Music and dance enthusiasts will enjoy a night out at one of Bangkok's many fantastic clubs. Electronic dance music aficionados will be delighted by Bangkok's various club choices, as will tourists seeking for a fantastic spot to hang out, relax, and party, since the city has several clubs to satisfy a wide range of preferences. With so many fantastic places to visit, the toughest part is deciding which one to attend for the night, but this list of five of Bangkok's greatest clubs will help tourists select which spots are perfect for them.

1. Sing sing Theater

Sing Sing Theater is an excellent choice for those searching for a nightclub that is a bit different from the others. Sing Sing Theater, with its strange, Chinese-themed décor, hosts some of Bangkok's best nighttime entertainment. Visitors visiting Bangkok can check out the event schedule at Sing Sing Theater to catch top DJs, dancers, and special events.

2. Maggie Choo

Maggie Choo's, with its speakeasy-style, delivers outstanding cuisine, interesting beverages, and fantastic entertainment for its patrons. Beautiful girls (and sometimes guys on "SunGay" evenings) hang from the ceiling in this unusual setting, entertaining visitors as they eat and drink. Maggie Choo's is a must-visit for those searching for a cabaret-style experience in Bangkok. This trendy bar, located on the basement floor of Novotel Bangkok Silom Road, is easily accessible to hotel guests.

3. Do Not Disturb (DND)

DND is a fantastic venue for experiencing Bangkok nightlife. DND customers may enjoy the ambience at this Bangkok club, which is known for its outstanding cuisine and amazing EDM music. DND, with its distinctive retro motel décor and vintage details, is the ideal place to get a bite to eat, relax with a beverage, and take in the sights and sounds of this one-of-a-kind club. At DND, customers often buy a bottle of alcohol for the evening rather than individual drinks, and the bottle order includes complimentary mixers. This technique might also help customers get a table at this renowned club.

What to Wear to Enjoy Bangkok's Nightlife

Visitors should dress semi-formally with excellent shoes before venturing out to experience Bangkok's nightlife. While unique dress rules may differ depending on the destination, it is preferable to dress too formally than not formally enough. If tourists want to spend the night exploring the night markets, they should dress casually, but they should dress up if they plan to attend clubs, bars, or other nightlife attractions. Bangkok is a cosmopolitan city with numerous world-class nightlife spots, therefore tourists should dress appropriately since they may enjoy better treatment throughout their night out if they seem properly dressed.

Chapter 11

VISITING BANGKOK WITH FAMILY

Family-friendly Activities

Bangkok boasts a plethora of family-friendly activities that children will enjoy. them vary from aquariums and theme parks to interactive art galleries and spectacular live events - you could spend a whole holiday with them and no one in the family would be bored.

There are also 'edutainment' locations where children may learn while playing, gaming arcades, and thrilling outdoor activities. There is just as much excitement and adventure for the kids as there is for mom and dad, and the options are limitless. This list includes the finest activities to do in Bangkok for families with children, as well as an age range to help you choose which ideas are appropriate. Check out what the big metropolis has to offer in terms of kid-friendly activities below.

1. Dream World (3 years and older)

Phone: +66 (0)2 577 8666

Dream World theme park is a fun-filled, exciting day out where, as the name implies, children's wishes become reality. In a single day, they can enjoy sledding and making snow angels in Snow Land, experience the thrill of riding a rollercoaster up Space Mountain, and have the opportunity to meet both Cinderella and Pocahontas.

While Dream World's high-octane rides may not be up to the standards of the top American or Japanese theme parks, the sights and activities for younger children are fantastic, ensuring an enjoyable family day out and plenty of unforgettable images.

2. Muay Thai Live (5 years and older)

Muay Thai Live is an amazing theatrical production that combines engaging acts with the traditional martial art of Muay Thai boxing at Asiatique Bangkok. The presentation, which is ideal for a family outing, enables everyone to experience the martial art behind the blood sport and is considerably more acceptable for smaller children than a true prize fight. There are lots of stores and restaurants to explore before or after the event at Asiatique Night Market

3. Siam Wonderful Park (3 years and older)

Waterparks are few in Bangkok, owing to the city's tropical environment. The finest site by far is Siam Amazing Park, which is becoming older but still entertaining. Children experience the greatest joy when they have the freedom to play, splash, wade, dive, and slide on slippery slides, while parents can either relax in the shade or join in the fun. There are thrilling rides and swimming pools for all types of water babies. There is also a separate amusement park with several exciting attractions for younger children.

4. Fantasia Lagoon (3 years and older)

Fantasia Lagoon is a reasonably sized and appealing waterpark erected on the roof of The Mall Bangkae, which is situated across the river on Bangkok's Thonburi side. Despite being accessible for many years, the park is fairly unknown to tourists, with the majority of visitors being Thai residents.

With large pools and decent-sized slides, Fantasia Lagoon is a wonderful spot for youngsters and young people to spend the day. You also get access to the full mall, including a cool gaming zone situated just underneath the water park.

5. Kidzania (3 to 12 years old)

Kidzania is Bangkok's most inventive addition to the 'edutainment' scene. It raises the amount of pleasure by enabling youngsters to participate in a variety of activities in a model city. Popular 'jobs' include pretending to be a doctor at the small hospital, putting out fires, police the streets, and learning how to cook sushi like a master chef. This is one of the simplest places to find in Bangkok, located in the Siam Paragon shopping mall, and there are lots of other exciting things to do nearby.

Kid-Friendly Attractions

Bangkok offers a variety of kid-friendly attractions and activities that are sure to keep children entertained and engaged. These are some well known Bangkok kid-friendly attractions:

1. Dusit Zoo (Khao Din Zoo):
Dusit Zoo is the oldest zoo in Thailand and a great place for children to see a wide range of animals, including elephants, lions, giraffes, and more. The zoo also features a playground and a mini-train ride, making it a fun day out for kids.

2. Siam Ocean World:
Located in Siam Paragon shopping mall, Siam Ocean World is one of Southeast Asia's largest aquariums. Kids can enjoy exploring various marine habitats and viewing fascinating sea creatures, including sharks, rays, and colorful fish.

3. Children's Discovery Museum:
The Children's Discovery Museum is an interactive museum that allows kids to engage in hands-on learning experiences. It features exhibits on science, technology, and culture, promoting curiosity and exploration.

4. Safari World:
Safari World is a combination of a drive-through safari park and a marine park. Kids can have close encounters with animals during the safari tour and

enjoy entertaining shows featuring dolphins, sea lions, and more.

5. Flow House Bangkok:

Flow House is an indoor surf center where kids can learn to surf or bodyboard on an artificial wave. It's a fun and safe way for children to experience surfing in the heart of the city.

6. Funarium:

Funarium is an indoor play center featuring a wide range of activities, including climbing walls, slides, trampolines, and a giant play structure. It's an excellent place for kids to burn off energy and have fun.

7. Playgrounds and Parks:

Bangkok has several parks and playgrounds where kids can enjoy outdoor activities. Lumpini Park, Benjasiri Park, and Queen Sirikit Park are popular choices for families.

With these kid-friendly attractions, Bangkok offers a wealth of fun and educational experiences for young visitors and their families. Whether exploring wildlife, engaging in role-play, or enjoying thrilling rides, children are sure to have a memorable time in the city.

CHAPTER 12

BANGKOK ITINERARIES AND TRIP IDEAS

Bangkok offers a plethora of exciting experiences and cultural delights for every type of traveler. Whether you're a history buff, a food enthusiast, a shopaholic, or a nature lover, Bangkok has something to offer. Here are diverse itineraries to help you make the most of your visit:

1-day Bangkok itinerary

Morning:
- Start your day with a visit to the Grand Palace, a majestic complex showcasing Thai architectural brilliance and housing the revered Temple of the Emerald Buddha (Wat Phra Kaew).

- Explore the intricate details of the temple's stunning murals and ornate decorations, immersing yourself in Thailand's rich cultural heritage.

Late Morning:
- Take a short walk to Wat Pho, the Temple of the Reclining Buddha. Marvel at the 46-meter-long golden Buddha statue, one of the largest in Thailand.

- Experience a traditional Thai massage at Wat Pho, where the ancient art of healing is practiced by skilled therapists.

Lunch:
- Head to a nearby street food market or local eatery to indulge in authentic Thai cuisine. Sample popular dishes like Pad Thai, Som Tum (green papaya salad), and Tom Yum Goong (spicy shrimp soup).

Afternoon:
- Visit the bustling and vibrant Chinatown (Yaowarat) area. Stroll through its bustling streets, filled with shops, street vendors, and Chinese temples.

- Explore the bustling markets and narrow alleys, where you can find unique souvenirs, clothing, and accessories.

Evening:
- As the sun sets, make your way to Asiatique The Riverfront, a lively night market with a wide range of shopping, dining, and entertainment options.

- Enjoy a scenic dinner at one of the riverside restaurants, offering stunning views of the Chao Phraya River.

Night:
- End your day with a relaxing river cruise along the Chao Phraya River, passing by illuminated landmarks and iconic temples.

7-Day Itinerary in Bangkok

Day 1: Arrival and City Orientation
- Arrive in Bangkok and check into your hotel.

- Spend the day getting familiar with the city. Take a leisurely stroll along Sukhumvit Road, exploring the vibrant street life and trying out local street food.

Day 2: Historical Landmarks

- Visit the Grand Palace and Wat Phra Kaew in the morning to witness the architectural splendor and spiritual significance of these iconic landmarks.

- Explore the nearby Wat Pho and enjoy a traditional Thai massage to relax and rejuvenate.

Day 3: Art and Culture

- Visit the Jim Thompson House, a beautifully preserved traditional Thai teakwood house showcasing art and artifacts.

- Head to the National Museum to delve deeper into Thailand's rich history and cultural heritage.

Day 4: Floating Market and River Cruise

- Take a day trip to Damnoen Saduak Floating Market or Amphawa Floating Market to experience the enchanting floating market culture.

- Enjoy a relaxing afternoon river cruise along the Chao Phraya River, passing by iconic landmarks and temples.

Day 5: Family Fun

- Spend the day at Siam Ocean World, an impressive aquarium with interactive exhibits and marine life.

- Visit KidZania Bangkok, where kids can engage in role-playing activities and explore various professions.

Day 6: Shopping and Culinary Delights

- Explore Chatuchak Weekend Market, one of the largest markets in the world, offering a vast array of goods, from clothing to handicrafts.

- Join a Thai cooking class to learn how to prepare authentic dishes, followed by a delightful dinner with your freshly cooked creations.

Day 7: Day of Relaxation

- Pamper yourself with a traditional Thai spa treatment or indulge in a day of shopping at modern shopping malls like Siam Paragon and CentralWorld.

- In the evening, visit Asiatique The Riverfront for some last-minute shopping and enjoy a farewell dinner with a scenic view of the Chao Phraya River.

History Lovers Itinerary

Day 1: Arrival and City Orientation

- Arrive in Bangkok and check into your hotel.

- Start your historical journey with a visit to the Bangkok National Museum, home to an extensive collection of artifacts and exhibits that chronicle Thailand's history.

Day 2: Grand Palace and Wat Pho
- Explore the Grand Palace, a magnificent complex that served as the royal residence for centuries. Admire the intricate architecture and intricate details of the buildings.

- Visit Wat Pho, known for its impressive Reclining Buddha statue and the oldest public university in Thailand.

Day 3: Ayutthaya Day Trip
- Take a day trip to Ayutthaya, the former capital of the Kingdom of Siam. Explore the Ayutthaya Historical Park, a UNESCO World Heritage Site, and marvel at the ancient temples and ruins.

Day 4: Jim Thompson House and Museum
- Discover the Jim Thompson House, a fascinating museum showcasing Thai art and architecture. Learn about the mysterious life of Jim Thompson, an American who played a significant role in reviving Thai silk.

Day 5: Ancient City (Muang Boran)

- Visit the Ancient City (Muang Boran), an open-air museum replicating Thailand's historical and cultural landmarks. Explore the sprawling grounds and witness replicas of ancient temples and structures.

Day 6: Wat Arun and City Pillar Shrine

- Visit Wat Arun, also known as the Temple of Dawn, famous for its stunning spires and riverside location.

- Pay a visit to the City Pillar Shrine, a sacred site dedicated to the guardian spirit of Bangkok.

Day 7: Bang Pa-In Royal Palace and Bang Krachao

- Explore Bang Pa-In Royal Palace, a beautiful summer palace with a mix of Thai, Chinese, and European architectural styles.

- Take a bike tour or boat ride to Bang Krachao, known as the "Green Lung" of Bangkok, and experience the serene beauty of the mangrove forests and local communities.

Food Lovers Itinerary

Day 1: Arrival and Local Street Food
- Arrive in Bangkok and check into your hotel.

- Start your culinary adventure with a walk along the lively Sukhumvit Road, where you can sample a variety of local street food delights.

Day 2: Thai Cooking Class
- Join a Thai cooking class to learn the secrets behind authentic Thai dishes like Pad Thai, Green Curry, and Som Tum.

- Enjoy the fruits of your labor as you feast on the dishes you prepared during the class.

Day 3: Floating Market and Local Specialties
- Take a day trip to Damnoen Saduak Floating Market or Amphawa Floating Market to savor traditional Thai dishes and snacks sold from boats.

- In the evening, explore Yaowarat (Chinatown) and indulge in a wide range of Chinese-Thai delicacies.

Day 4: Food Markets and Street Food

- Visit the bustling Or Tor Kor Market to taste an array of fresh tropical fruits, local snacks, and street food delights.

- Experience the vibrant atmosphere and unique flavors of Rod Fai Ratchada Night Market or Talad Neon Night Market.

Day 5: Fine Dining Experience

- Treat yourself to a fine dining experience at a riverside restaurant, offering a blend of authentic Thai and international cuisine.

- Enjoy a romantic dinner with stunning views of the Chao Phraya River.

Day 6: Michelin-Starred Restaurants

- Explore Bangkok's culinary scene further by visiting Michelin-starred restaurants, known for their exceptional dishes and innovative flavors.

Day 7: Foodie Adventures and Departure

- Embark on a foodie adventure in the morning, exploring hidden gems in the city or visiting trendy cafes and dessert spots.
- Before departing, indulge in one last meal of delectable Thai dishes, reminiscing about your delightful food journey in Bangkok.

Itinerary for Family

Day 1: Arrival and Relaxation
- Arrive in Bangkok and check into your family-friendly hotel.

- Spend the day relaxing by the hotel pool or exploring the nearby parks, such as Lumpini Park, where kids can enjoy playgrounds and boat rides.

Day 2: Siam Ocean World and Shopping
- Head to Siam Paragon to visit Siam Ocean World, a massive aquarium featuring interactive exhibits and marine life.

- After the aquarium, indulge in some family shopping and enjoy a delicious meal at the mall's diverse food court.

Day 3: KidZania Bangkok and Funarium

- Spend the day at KidZania Bangkok, an interactive city where kids can role-play various professions, from doctors to firefighters.

- In the afternoon, visit Funarium, an indoor play center with climbing walls, trampolines, and more for endless family fun.

Day 4: Bangkok Zoo and Dusit Park

- Explore Dusit Zoo, home to a variety of animals, including elephants and lions. Kids will enjoy the zoo's playful atmosphere.

- After the zoo, visit Dusit Park, a peaceful green space with large open fields, perfect for a family picnic.

Day 5: Dream World Amusement Park

- Embark on a thrilling adventure at Dream World, an amusement park with exciting rides, shows, and themed areas for all ages.

- End the day with a delightful dinner at the park's food outlets.

Day 6: Safari World and Marine Park

- Experience the wildlife wonders at Safari World, where you can embark on a safari tour to see animals in their natural habitats.

- Enjoy a spectacular show at Marine Park, featuring dolphins, sea lions, and more.

Day 7: Relaxing Spa Treatments and Departure

- Treat the family to a relaxing spa session, offering family-friendly treatments like foot massages or gentle oil massages.

- Before departing, cherish the memories of your family adventures in Bangkok and bid the city farewell.

Conclusion

In the enchanting realm of Bangkok, where the past whispers through ornate temples and the future roars with the pace of a vibrant metropolis, travelers are beckoned to embark on an unforgettable journey. From the tranquil waters of the Chao Phraya River to the bustling markets that ignite all senses, Bangkok is a symphony of contrasts, seamlessly blending tradition with modernity. As you wander its bustling streets and hidden alleys, the city will weave its spell around you, capturing your heart with every smile and leaving an indelible imprint on your soul. So, embrace the energy, savor the flavors, and immerse yourself in the rich tapestry of Bangkok – a city that celebrates life with unbridled passion, inviting you to dance in its rhythm and create memories that will linger long after you bid it farewell. As the sun sets over the majestic skyline, you'll find that Bangkok's true allure lies not just in its shimmering façade but in the profound connection it fosters, turning strangers into kindred spirits. Prepare to be enchanted, for in Bangkok, dreams take flight, and the possibilities are boundless. Discover this world of wonders, and let the heart of Thailand welcome you home.

Printed in Great Britain
by Amazon